CENSORS IN THE CLASSROOM

The
Mind Benders

By
Edward B. Jenkinson

SOUTHERN ILLINOIS
UNIVERSITY PRESS
Carbondale and Edwardsville
Feffer & Simons, Inc.
London and Amsterdam

To my wife, Ronna, and to our children—
Mark, Andrea, and Nicholas

To Judy Krug and the Office for Intellectual
Freedom of the American Library Association

To all teachers who have experienced
attempts at censorship

Copyright © 1979 by Southern Illinois University Press
All rights reserved
Printed in the United States of America
Designed by Gary Gore

Library of Congress Cataloging in Publication Data

Jenkinson, Edward B
  Censors in the classroom.

  Includes bibliographical references and index.
  1. Text-books—United States—Censorship. I. Title.
LB3047.J46   379'.156   79-17417
ISBN 0-8093-0929-7

Contents

Acknowledgments

To complete a book on a controversial subject like censorship, a writer needs constant encouragement and support from friends and relatives. I received both from my family—to whom this book is dedicated—and from James Simmons, Assistant Director and Editor of the Southern Illinois University Press, who suggested that I write this book and who gently persuaded me to keep returning to the research and to the typewriter until the manuscript was completed.

Any person who writes about current censorship activity in the schools discovers that the task would be extremely difficult if it were not for the *Newsletter on Intellectual Freedom* of the American Library Association. Grateful acknowledgment is given to Judith F. Krug and Roger L. Funk, Director and Assistant Director, respectively, of the Office for Intellectual Freedom of the ALA, for their *Newsletter,* their help, and their encouragement.

The following people sent me newspaper clippings, copies of articles and/or legal briefs, firsthand accounts of censorship activities, and/or hundreds of words of support: Theodora Baer, Bellevue, Washington; Teresa Burnau, Warsaw, Indiana; JoAnn DuPont, Warsaw, Indiana; Edmund Farrell, University of Texas at Austin; Donald Grove, Volga, Iowa; Dale Harris, Indiana State Teachers Association; Susan Heath, Nicolet College and Technical Institute, Rhinelander, Wisconsin; Robert Spencer Johnson, Glen Cove, New York; Leanne Katz, National Coalition Against Censorship; John Maxwell, National Council of Teachers of English; Donald Messimer, Mifflinburg, Pennsylvania; Thomas Nenneman, Omaha, Nebraska; Robert O'Neil, Indiana University, Bloomington; Charles Park, University of Wisconsin at Whitewater; Everett S. Porter, North-

Acknowledgments

east Missouri State University, Kirksville, Missouri; Robert Rhode, Indiana University, Bloomington; Paul Slayton, Mary Washington College, Fredericksburg, Virginia; and Tony and Jackie Zykan, Warsaw, Indiana.

The following members of the Committee Against Censorship of the National Council of Teachers of English read versions of several chapters in this book as they were prepared for professional journals: Gertrude Berger, Brooklyn College; Lee Burress, University of Wisconsin at Stevens Point; Gary Cox, Kokomo, Indiana; James Davis, Ohio University at Athens; Ken Donelson, Arizona State University at Tempe; and Diane Shugert, Central Connecticut State College.

Mere words cannot express my appreciation for the work of Kathi Lee and Julie Bobay of Bloomington, Indiana, for their careful typing of the manuscript, their help with the proofreading, and their invaluable assistance with the index.

Portions of chapter 1 were based, in part, on these articles that I submitted to professional journals: " 'Who Will Control the Minds of the Students' in Warsaw, Indiana?" *Occasional Paper 16,* The Indiana Council of Teachers of English, November 1978, and "The New Wave of Censorship Hits an Indiana Town," *Newsletter on Intellectual Freedom,* May 1979. Portions of chapters 5 and 6 were based, in part, on these articles that I submitted to professional journals or books: "What Will Be Left to Censor in 1984?" *Focus: The Teaching English Language Arts,* Fall 1977; "The Mind-Benders: Censorship in the Classroom," *The Hoosier Schoolmaster,* Winter 1979; "Dirty Dictionaries, Obscene Nursery Rhymes, and Burned Books," *Dealing with Censorship* (James E. Davis, Editor), Urbana: National Council of Teachers of English, 1979; "How to Keep Dictionaries Out of the Public Schools," *Verbatim,* Spring 1979. Portions of chapter 8 were based, in part, on these articles that I submitted to professional journals or books: "How to Condemn a Book Without Reading It," *Newsletter on Intellectual Freedom,* May 1978; "How the Mel Gablers Have Put Textbooks on Trial," *Dealing with Censorship* (James E. Davis, Editor), Urbana: National Council of Teachers of English, 1979.

Grateful acknowledgment is also given to Robert T. Rhode, whose article on secular humanism published in Edward B.

Acknowledgments

Jenkinson, Editor, *Organized Censors Rarely Rest* (Terre Haute: Indiana Council of Teachers of English, 1977) was immensely helpful as I attempted to write chapter 7.

Nearly all of the quoted material in this book was taken from mimeographed handouts, membership brochures, bills of particulars that are a matter of public record, mimeographed newsletters or letters to concerned parents, printed and duplicated newsletters that are not copyrighted, advertisements, legal briefs and decisions, and newspaper clippings. Grateful acknowledgment is given to the writers of that material, which constitutes a significant portion of this book.

Finally, grateful acknowledgment is extended to the following individuals and organizations for permission to reprint specific information: The American Humanist Association for portions of *Humanist Manifesto II,* reprinted on pages 103–4; Ken Donelson for the quotation from "Censorship: Some Issues and Problems," *Theory into Practice,* June 1975, reprinted on pages 71–72; Dorothy C. Massie, Inquiry Specialist for the National Education Association, for the quotations from *Kanawha County West Virginia: A Textbook Study in Cultural Conflict* (Washington, D.C.: National Education Association, 1975), reprinted on pages 24–27; Onalee McGraw, Education Consultant for The Heritage Foundation, for three quotations from her *Secular Humanism and the Schools: The Issue Whose Time Has Come* (Washington, D.C.: The Heritage Foundation, 1976), reprinted on pages 97, 127, and 133; for one quotation from the September 1977 issue of *Education Update,* reprinted on pages 132–33; and for one quotation from her *Family Choice in Education: The New Imperative* (Washington, D.C.: The Heritage Foundation, 1978), reprinted on page 133. The Scripture Press for the quotation from James C. Hefley's *Textbooks on Trial,* (Wheaton, Ill.: Victor Books, 1976), reprinted on page 97; John Steinbacher, formerly of Educator Publications, for permission to reprint the quotation from "To Capture a Nation—Change the Religion," reprinted on page 98, and for the quotation from Mary Royer's "Humanism—a clear-cut philosophy," reprinted on pages 97–98; *The Wilson Library Bulletin* for a quotation from Lester Asheim's "Not Censorship but Selection," September 1953, reprinted on page 72.

Introduction

"You call yourself a Christian, but you're not. You're an atheist, a communist, and a smut peddler. Why do you insist on having children read four-letter words in school? Why do you want to fill their minds with trash? Why do you want to destroy America's children?"

The words in that paragraph from an unsigned letter to me are not new, but they still sting. I received that letter, and a few others like it, several days after I appeared on a popular television program to express my opposition to the organizations that are attempting to censor school textbooks and other teaching materials. I reread that letter to remind myself of the sentiments of people who believe that all public school textbooks are filled with smut and violence or with ideas that will turn students away from God, country, parents, authority, and virtue. Occasionally, I share the words in that paragraph with teachers and administrators who have experienced the wrath of the censors. I am no longer surprised when the victims of censorship tell me that the words in the paragraph are so common that they are probably part of a form letter prepared by anyone of dozens of organizations that give textbook protesters advice on what to censor and how to go about it.

When I began studying attempts to censor school materials in the early seventies, I thought that most would-be censors were individual parents acting alone to protest a book they did not want their children to read. I soon learned that my assumption, based on my own experiences as a classroom teacher in the fifties and as a college instructor working with teachers in the sixties, was open to challenge. Individual parents still protest books, but many of them today do so with the advice of one or more of at least two hundred organizations in this nation that want to change the public schools. The number of parents protesting books has increased markedly during the last decade, and the number of incidents of attempted censorship has nearly tripled. Both the methods and the targets of the censors have changed since the fifties and sixties, and it is worth considering some of the causes for the changes.

As a beginning teacher in the fifties, I infrequently heard about parents who called teachers or visited the principal to complain about a book. But the incidents were rare. My colleagues and I chuckled when an elected official condemned *Robin Hood* because it was allegedly communistic, and we spent an hour amusing ourselves by trying to think of as many books as we could with red or pink in the title that could become a target of the legislator. We knew that we had little to fear in our own classrooms. Most parents were not worried about what their sons and daughters were reading in the early fifties, for they knew that books for teenagers dealt with safe topics in sterile language.

As an English teacher, I was assigned to teach grammar one semester and literature the next. The literature provoked few comments from parents since most of us used anthologies that were revised editions of the ones the parents had studied years before. Across the hall the history teachers taught from books that focused on dates and recounted the major events in the history of a nation that seemingly could do little wrong. Down the hall the biology and health teachers taught units on human reproduction that sometimes drew criticism, but few parents became upset enough to protest the line drawings of human reproductive organs. Academic freedom was not a common topic of discussion in the teachers' lounge, and I can recall only one teacher who talked about it. He was sorely troubled by the national organizations that joined forces to censor two series of history textbooks before and after World War II, and he talked passionately about the need for both teachers of English and history to discuss controversial issues with students. Most of us agreed with him, but we rarely departed from the assigned textbooks. They were safe.

The teacher who strayed from the textbook to assign additional readings or to discuss issues raised by the students might discover that people outside the classroom had ways of finding out what was said and done in class. But the complainants rarely demanded that the offending teacher be dismissed. In fact, a teacher did not always learn about a complaint if the principal could handle it without difficulty. That was true in my case. As a beginning teacher in a country school, I encouraged my students to visit the county library and check out a variety of books. Two years after I left that school for a teaching position in a nearby city, I learned that several parents and a minister had complained about the books my students were reading. But no one in the school told me about the protest because no colleague or interested parent wanted me to stop encouraging my students to read. Other teachers were not always so fortunate. If they introduced controversial ideas or if they included controversial books on their reading lists, they might have been reprimanded or even—in extreme cases—dismissed. For the most part, however, school was a safe place in which noncontroversial books and ideas were discussed in classes in which most teachers used only tried and tested teaching methods. Then Holden Caulfield checked into school.

After *The Catcher in the Rye* captured the attention of teachers, librarians, and students, talk of censorship became more common in teachers' lounges. Newspapers reported incidents in which school officials forbade the antics of Holden to be read and discussed; they also reported that some school board members and administrators found nothing obscene in *The Catcher* and approved it for use in classrooms.

Hard on the heels of *The Catcher* came scores of paperback books that focused on real problems that troubled teenagers. By the late sixties, publishers were no longer reluctant to release books about life as young people experienced it in language that teenagers frequently used. Teachers who were searching for books that reluctant readers might try to read began assigning novels that students liked to read and discuss. Some parents who were accustomed only to noncontroversial novels written in genteel language began protesting.

Suddenly parents who wanted the schools to return to the

good old days could find many reasons to be alarmed. Students and teachers alike protested against the war in Vietnam. School textbooks challenged some of the actions and decisions of historical figures. Historical dates were no longer memorized. Instead, students discussed and debated issues and they demanded that their courses be relevant. Schools changed. Small schools disappeared and large, consolidated schools replaced them. Students boarded buses before daybreak to ride to the nearest school. The courts began enforcing the 1954 Supreme Court decision that blacks need not be forced to attend separate schools, and school buses began transporting students for the purpose of integration.

The schools continued to change. Some were constructed without inner walls. Parents heard speeches about the merits of open schools and open classrooms. Some schools did away with the 50-minute class period and replaced it with flexible scheduling. Teachers taught in teams. Students could even ask for individualized programs. The new math caught parents offguard, and many discovered that they could no longer help their children with their homework. English became less traditional; innovative educators replaced the semester of grammar with two nine-week courses they called part of a "phase-elective" program. Sex education courses became part of the curriculum, and drug education courses were introduced in an effort to counter the drug culture. Educators talked about programs designed to make schools exciting places that prepared students for "the real world." The United States Office of Education awarded millions of dollars to schools and colleges to develop and test new programs. Values clarification became an accepted term in some communities, and many parents applauded the new programs.

But throughout the period of change, critics of education protested some school programs or actions of the educators. They decried the removal of prayer from the schools. Some maintained that the discovery or inquiry methods used in social studies classes were permitting students to challenge the decisions of the nation's leaders and thus to become less patriotic. Others claimed that the schools were encouraging students to question the values of their parents and of their churches. The media announced that test scores were declining, that the new math was a failure, that Johnny could neither read nor write well, that violence and vandalism were rampant in the schools, that open schools did not always work, that the cost of education kept rising as a result of teachers' demanding more money without guaranteeing a better education for students, and that concerned parents were clamoring for private schools. Back to the basics became a battlecry heard throughout the land. And more and more parents joined together to form organizations through which they could complain about the schools in general and textbooks in particular.

During the last decade, citizens concerned about the public schools have formed at least two hundred organizations at the local, state, and national levels. Some want to change the public schools by removing textbooks and courses they consider offensive; others claim that the schools are beyond hope and that concerned parents must build their own private schools if they want their children to have a decent education. Nearly all of the organizations want to remove from the schools those books, teaching materials, and courses they consider to be anti-God, anti-parent, anti-country, or immoral. Those seem to be noble goals which every parent can endorse. But close examination reveals that the fulfillment of those goals could destroy the student's right to know and to read as well as the teacher's right to teach.

Myths and legends and some fairy tales could be labeled anti-God. The examination of the cultures of the world could lead students into an exploration of pagan cultures which are, of course, anti-God. The study of the humanities is sometimes perceived as being anti-God because students explore the achievements and problems of man without always acknowledging God. Throughout this book I provide examples of attacks on materials that are labeled anti-God. In fact, many of the protesting organizations accuse the entire public school system of teaching secular humanism or atheistic humanism, which they claim is a religion that is anti-God. (See chapter 7.)

The organizations that would change the schools object to

stories about conflicts between students and parents. They object to any sentence in a story which indicates that parents are not perfect. They object to assignments that ask students to examine conflicts between teenagers and adults. The organized censors do not want students to read about the mistakes this country's leaders may have made. Nor do they want children to study the lives and beliefs of such prominent figures as Martin Luther King, Jr., Cesar Chavez, Malcolm X, and Chief Crazy Horse. Nor do they want attention paid to the Vietnam War or to Watergate, for they seem to fear that when students become aware of these problems they will develop anti-country attitudes.

Finally, the censors believe that students should not read books that are immoral. Every parent in America might agree with that. On the other hand, not every parent would agree that *Drums Along the Mohawk* is obscene because it contains a few *hells* and *damns*. Nor would every parent agree with the charge that *Go Ask Alice* is pornography. That book contains street language, but it does not shock most students. Rather, according to students who have talked with me about the book, it shocks and frightens them because of what happened to a young girl as a result of using drugs. The students understand that she uses the language of the street when she's hooked on drugs; otherwise, she avoids such language. Students have told me that they consider *Go Ask Alice* to be a very moral book because it, in its own way, upholds high moral standards. Yet in community after community in the United States, *Go Ask Alice* has been removed from libraries and classrooms—frequently by parents and school officials who have not even bothered to read the entire book before condemning it.

Anyone who dares speak out for a book like *Go Ask Alice* or *Flowers for Algernon* or *Black Boy* should know that the censors will call him or her a smut peddler, a corrupter of youth, a scum, an atheist, and perhaps even a communist. In addition to those epithets, I have been called the "champion of street language and explicit sex" in the classroom. Nothing could be further from the truth. I, too, am a censor. I do not permit my daughter to watch certain television shows because they are filled with

xvi

crime and violence. I do not want her to read certain literary works because I believe that she is not yet ready for them. As a parent, I feel that I have a moral obligation to be concerned about what my child sees and reads. On the other hand, I know I do not have the right to impose my standards on the other children in her class or in the nation. I must live with the constant uncertainty that by denying her the right to read or see anything that I may be seriously limiting her education. I do not know exactly what is best for my child—I can only try to provide what I think is right. But the public censor apparently knows what is best for all children.

I first became aware of the public censor's assumed omniscience as I read about the battle of the books in Kanawha County, West Virginia. Reading reports of that series of confrontations over textbooks prompted me to begin studying the nationwide movement to censor materials in the public schools, to discredit them, and, perhaps, to destroy them. I have listened to ministers say on national television: "We must bring immoral public education to its knees." I have read articles urging parents to withdraw their children from public schools because they are being taught the religion of secular humanism. I have read articles about how parents can start their own schools, and I have read hundreds of pages of reviews of textbooks used in the public schools. I frequently could not believe what I was reading.

About five years ago, more and more of the classroom teachers I work with throughout Indiana began talking with me about attempts by individuals and groups to censor certain books. Several teachers asked me to help them retain their teaching materials, methods, and courses. I quickly learned that if I planned to help I needed to understand the tactics of the censors and to be able to identify their targets.

Then three years ago, the Executive Committee of the National Council of Teachers of English asked me to serve as chairman of its newly formed Committee on Censorship. After I received letters congratulating me for accepting a position that would give me the opportunity to censor books, I asked NCTE's Executive Committee to change the name of the group to Committee Against Censorship so that the title would not be misleading. As chairman of the committee, I learned in a very short time that attempts to censor school materials are increasing yearly and that teachers under attack have few sources of help. Only the American Library Association's Office for Intellectual Freedom devotes its full time to combatting censorship. Other professional organizations have committees like NCTE's, but committees that work part time cannot be of great help to beleaguered teachers. For coping with the censors can consume every waking hour of the day if one permits it to do so. And coping with the censors requires a thorough knowledge of their tactics and targets.

During the last three years, I have spent countless hours reading textbook reviews written by censors. I have read dozens of their articles and monographs as well as their battle plans for ridding the schools of books they consider evil. I have also spent hours talking with people who would censor school materials. I have appeared on television shows with them, and I have participated in radio debates. I have read their proposed legislation, and I have written letters opposing it. I have spent days in a community under attack by censors, and I have spent hours talking with a number of the participants in that drama. I have tried to learn what the current censorship movement is all about.

This book is the result of my study of recent attempts at censorship. In it I do not attempt to trace the history of censorship. Rather, I focus on censorship incidents that have occurred in public schools since Kanawha County's story was reported in newspapers from coast to coast in 1974. The three incidents reported in this book that are exceptions to that dateline occurred only months before the Kanawha County tragedy began.

I have tried neither to speak for the censors nor to intrude my views on what they were doing, but to let them speak for themselves by quoting from their publications, their reviews, their articles, or the newspaper accounts of what they have done. It should be clear to the reader that although I disagree with the position many censors take, I recognize their right to do what they are doing. They have every right to complain, to protest, to air their views. I balk only when their actions encroach upon the student's right to know and the teacher's right to teach.

The censors have been successful in many instances because parents do not always take the time to read the books under attack, or to attend school board meetings, or to talk with teachers about their courses and course objectives. When parents do take the time, they frequently champion what the schools are doing and decry the work of the censors. The positive support of parents depends, to a great extent, on the willingness of educators to explain programs to all parents and to do so without resorting to jargon. When educators meet with concerned parents, such controversial programs as values clarification and drug education usually stay in the curriculum especially if the curriculum committee has parent representatives.

Thorough knowledge of so-called objectionable materials frequently leads to their defense. A concerned parent who actually reads an objectionable work or studies descriptions of offensive courses may find little that is objectionable or offensive particularly if that parent wants children to be able to think for themselves, to read widely and freely, and to be able to make wise, informed decisions.

I have written this book as a concerned parent with deep religious convictions who hopes that my children will grow up free to read, free to think, free to challenge, and free to make their own decisions. I definitely do not believe that all books and films are worthy of study in a classroom; on the other hand, I do not think that a book or film should be thrown out because it offends the sensibilities of a few who may or may not have read the entire work or seen it. I have kept one quotation in mind: "Censorship is the tool of tyrannous societies."

Bloomington, Indiana
April, 1979

Censors in the Classroom

1

"WHO WILL CONTROL THE MINDS OF THE STUDENTS?"

Warsaw sits proudly atop the rich loam of northeastern Indiana. Characterized as a conservative community "with a strong religious feeling," the nearly ten thousand citizens of Warsaw have their choice of sixty-three churches, "mostly Protestant," in the immediate town area.[1] The people of Warsaw talk about their church-affiliated college on Winona Lake, their state championship high school girls' basketball team, their thriving small industries, and their phenomenally low rate of unemployment, which was reported to be 1.5 percent in the summer of 1978.[2] At one time they also talked enthusiastically about their public schools, but now they tend to be less animated in their conversations about the schools since a series of decisions by the school board and administrators prompted reporters from nationally prominent newspapers and television newscasters to enter their city.

One journalist reported that "this town's troubles have the dramatic elements of a modern play full of passion and moralizing. School textbooks are banned. Books are burned. A young teacher is fired. The local newspaper's editorials and letters to the editor are ablaze with sharp comment."[3] Another reporter wrote that the "book-burning here last winter was dramatic, but it was something more. It was symbolic of a new wave of controversy over books and educational films being used in the nation's public schools."[4]

The reporter's assessment is accurate. The Warsaw controversy did not stem from someone's attempt to ban a so-called dirty book or two as was the cause of so many battles over books in the late sixties and early seventies. The Warsaw situation is far more complex. It presages the problems that will arise whenever people turn the back-to-basics movement into a crusade. It also illustrates some—but not all—of the targets of the critics of today's schools: entire courses, teaching methods, entire programs, educational philosophies, as well as individual books. Finally, it reflects the increasingly prevalent attitude toward teachers and the belief that they do not enjoy academic freedom and that students have the right to learn only what their parents want them to. William I. Chapel, member of the Board of School Trustees of the Warsaw Community Schools, was quoted as saying: "The bottom line is: Who will control the minds of the students—parents and citizens of the community or some external force?"[5] Mr. Chapel was quoted by another reporter as commenting: "You keep mentioning the First Amendment. How does it apply to what we're doing?"[6]

Frustrated students, teachers, and parents in Warsaw believe that both the first and fourteenth amendments figure prominently in the school board's decisions to remove textbooks and courses from the schools. Several teachers and students have filed suits in federal courts to determine to what extent the school board and administrators violated their constitutional rights in a series of incidents that one teacher labeled "too bizarre to be believed if they were described in a novel. No one would believe what happened here if we couldn't document it through minutes of school board meetings and newspaper clippings."[7]

The Warsaw story began with the school board's decision to review the individually guided education program (IGE) at Washington Elementary School. According to a news story in

2

the *Warsaw Times-Union* on April 12, 1977, "Board members have been receiving numerous comments from Washington parent-patrons who say they disagree with certain aspects of the school's program and personnel."[8]

Washington is the only school in Kosciusko County that ever used the IGE packets developed at the University of Wisconsin. According to one Warsaw teacher, the program was a pet project of Superintendent Max E. Hobbs, and it had been in effect for five years. It had also become one of the targets of local, state, and national groups organized to exert pressure on public schools to ban objectionable textbooks, teaching materials, and teaching methods.

Early in May the *Times-Union* reported that three members of the school board would be part of a committee that "will officially review the elementary school's curriculum, which has come under fire from Washington parents who say their children are not learning basic skills such as reading, writing and arithmetic" under IGE.[9] Two weeks later the *Times-Union* noted that the school board had voted to have a professor from a state-supported university "thoroughly study Washington Elementary School"[10] during the last three days of school. People in Warsaw could not believe that any program could be studied effectively during the last week of a school year. According to the newspaper, even the supporters of IGE were incredulous.[11] So was Superintendent Max E. Hobbs, who announced his resignation after seven years in Warsaw.

On June 21, the school board met in special session for fifteen minutes and voted to drop the IGE program and to establish "strict parameters" in all nine elementary schools. "The board action standardizes curriculum and teaching methods in each elementary."[12] Three weeks later the school board announced the appointment of a new principal for the elementary school and the transfer of four of its teachers. An attorney representing 230 disgruntled parents of pupils at Washington protested the transfer, noting that the teachers were being penalized because they "at one time or another had spoken up in support of the system (IGE)."[13] The school board sustained the transfer.

3

After the school board disposed of IGE, it set its sights on another target that local, state, and national school pressure groups want to obliterate. The following paragraph was included in the minutes of the school board meeting for July 19, 1977: "A discussion was held on the Values Clarification class at the Senior High School. Mr. Chapel submitted for review the textbook used by the Values Clarification Class. After the Board reviewed the material submitted, and following a lengthy discussion about this class, Mr. [Fred] Yohey made a motion, seconded by Mrs. [Marie] Stokes, that the Values Clarification class at the Senior High School be dropped immediately from the English Department, and that the textbook used in this class be removed from the school premises immediately, with the understanding that the textbook used for this class will be destroyed when legally permissible."[14]

According to the *Times-Union,* "It took only a few minutes of reading passages from the text for the school board's reaction to throw the book out and discontinue the English class that once used it." Mr. Yohey stated in his motion that the book should be "thrown out, removed, banned, destroyed and forbidden to be used."[15]

In subsequent board meetings, teachers of English at the high school protested the action of the board. The teachers noted that the passages Mr. Chapel chose to read to the board were not used in the phase-elective English class. According to one former teacher, "only ten of the approximately two hundred exercises in the book were used in the class."[16] But according to the *Times-Union,* the board "banned the book last month because it contained passages that asked students to share their views on premarital sex, masturbation and other experiences. Board members said they believed exercises in the book could encourage students to reject their family values and those of churches, government and other institutions."[17]

The book in question is *Values Clarification* by Sidney B. Simon, Leland W. Howe, and Howard Kirschenbaum (New York: Hart Publishing Co., 1972). The book and the course became a part of the English curriculum after Dr. Max E. Hobbs,

4

the former superintendent, had invited the Indiana Department of Public Instruction to conduct an in-service training program on values clarification in August of 1975. As a result of that workshop and subsequent study, the English Department of Warsaw Community High School added a course entitled "Values for Everyone" to its elective program, and the teacher used parts of the book in the course. Other teachers in Warsaw were encouraged to study the approaches used in values clarification courses and to select whatever exercises they deemed appropriate for their own classes.

Nearly one month after the banning of the book, Mr. Chapel read excerpts of evaluations of the textbook by two practicing psychologists and asked that the evaluations become part of the minutes.[18] The next day the *Times-Union* devoted nine paragraphs to the reviews, but neither the newspaper nor Mr. Chapel identified the two psychologists who wrote the evaluations. On December 15, 1977, the *Times-Union* published a photograph of a group of senior citizens burning forty copies of *Values Clarification*.[19] During the height of the controversy over the banned textbook, Arleen Miner, coordinator for the Department of English at Warsaw Community High School and a teacher in Warsaw for thirty years, resigned her position as coordinator. Mrs. Miner told the school board that "there is not enough trust in me." She felt that she should have been consulted about the English program before the school board decided to change it. The school board had voted to replace three high school English classes with two composition courses. Mrs. Miner said that the school board had been misinformed when it was told there was only one writing course in the high school phase-elective program. "There are five writing courses," she said.[20]

The English curriculum had obviously been slated for major changes. On August 25, 1977, just forty-two days after he had been appointed superintendent, Dr. Charles Bragg announced the following changes, among others, in the English program, and his recommendations were unanimously approved by the school board.

1. the addition of these three courses to be offered starting September 5: Composition I (grammar and composition), Composition II (essay writing) and College Prep (developmental reading, college bound);

2. the discontinuation of the following courses in the second semester: Gothic Literature, Black Literature, Science Fiction, Good Guys, Folklore and Legends, Detective and Mystery Fiction, and Whatever Happened to Mankind;

3. the discontinuation of the phase-elective APEX program at the end of the 1977–78 school year;

4. the development, during the 1977–78 academic year, of a required English program for grades seven through eleven with elective offerings for grade twelve.[21]

Three teachers of English told me that they were quite apprehensive about starting the 1977–78 academic year since they were convinced that even more changes would be made in the English program. Their suspicions were soon confirmed. During the 1976–77 academic year, first year teacher Teresa Burnau had been assigned to teach a phase-elective course entitled "Women in Literature," which she taught from the outline designed by her predecessor. In the spring of her first year, Ms. Burnau, who had spent most of her life in Warsaw and who thought she recognized community standards, revised the course and asked the principal to order the books for the following year. Her original list included *The Stepford Wives, Go Ask Alice, The Bell Jar, Growing Up Female in America, The Feminine Plural: Stories by Women About Growing Up,* and *The New Women: A Motive Anthology of Women's Liberation.* When the books arrived at the beginning of the school year, Ms. Burnau reported that C. J. Smith, the principal, gave them a "cursory examination." He asked her to return *Growing Up Female in America* to the publisher because it contained pictures of nude women. She agreed to return the copies since the book was to be used as supplementary material.

Later that same day the principal asked Ms. Burnau to return to his office. He told her that *The Stepford Wives* was "of

6

questionable nature." Ms. Burnau added: "He pointed out that the women in the story discussed sleeping with their husbands. He did not know what the story was about, nor did he support my desire to use it. He simply dismissed the book because someone in the community might be offended." Ms. Burnau reported that she did express "a certain degree of frustration and anger" when she was told that she could not use *The Stepford Wives.* "I pointed out that even if Warsaw is a conservative community, there is a certain reality that must be recognized. That reality is that teenagers should deal with sexuality on an intellectual level rather than an emotional one. He did not deny what I said, but he removed the book from the course."

Nearly six weeks into the semester, Mr. Smith told Ms. Burnau to stop teaching *Go Ask Alice* because it "was found to be objectionable by patrons of our school."[22] When she told him that the girls in the class had nearly finished reading the book, she was told to let them read the rest of it. In a supervisor's conference report, the principal commented: "You were advised to discontinue the use of any reading materials that contained these kinds of obscenities. A guideline to follow is not to use any reading materials in your classes that would cause you embarrassment if you were asked to read these materials to our governing body."[23]

On the last day of November, Mr. Smith instructed Ms. Burnau not to use Sylvia Plath's *The Bell Jar* in her class. Ms. Burnau protested in writing, noting that it was too late for her to select and order another book. However, when she was told that she would be dismissed for insubordination if she taught the book, even though she offered to let any student choose an alternate one, she dropped the Plath autobiography.

When Mr. Smith filed his staff appraisal report on Ms. Burnau in March, he noted that she "is an excellent classroom teacher and is doing a fine job in teaching Composition I this second semester." He marked her as being satisfactory (the highest rating) on fourteen of eighteen items. He marked her as unsatisfactory on "continues to grow professionally." In his written comments, he noted that she had used a book, *Go Ask*

Alice, considered to be objectionable and that she displayed "resentment and a poor attitude" for not being able to use *The Bell Jar.*[24]

At the end of April, Ms. Burnau received a letter of dismissal from Superintendent Bragg. He noted her inability "to handle professional direction in a positive manner" and added that "there appears to be the lack of a continuum of growth in areas which involve maturity and judgment and acts on your part which indicate a lack of enthusiasm."[25]

Ms. Burnau was not the only Warsaw teacher who was dismissed in 1978. Eleven teachers were asked to resign; Ms. Burnau and two others refused and were dismissed. One of the dismissed teachers, JoAnn DuPont, had this statement included in an editorial in *KONTAC,* the high school student newspaper:

On Wednesday, April 12, five days before the Board terminated my contract, I was advised of the following reasons for my contract non-renewal: 1. drinking coffee in my room; 2. allowing my students to eat candy and drink pop at their desks; 3. being out of my room and the students not knowing where I was; and 4. allowing my daughter to allegedly be in my classroom when her bus brought her back from Sacred Heart at 2:49 p.m. Since I have not received any criticism of my teaching performance in the five years at Warsaw, and this year's was equally good, including phrases, "continues to do an effective job" and "conscientious" and "recommended for continued employment," I was shocked when Dr. Bragg gave me his letter stating Mr. Smith was recommending my contract not be renewed. This proves that the evaluation policy currently being used in all buildings is totally worthless. It also proves that this administration is not interested in the best performance from all teachers since they are not willing to identify weak areas, give specific recommendations for improvement, and a sufficient

4. [H-], the intellectual and cultural movement that stemmed from the study of classical Greek and Latin literature and culture during the Middle Ages and was one of the factors giving rise to the Renaissance; it was characterized by an emphasis on human interests rather than on the natural world or religion.

The compounding of those two words has resulted in a battle cry that echos throughout the land wherever organizations determined to change the public schools are heard. To their way of thinking, secular humanism will destroy youth and, ultimately, the United States. The organizations fear "evil" Secular Humanism, as these quotations illustrate:

The humanist educators have taken it upon themselves, without your consent, to change the attitudes of your children in regard to God, Family, and County [*sic*]. For example, most all social studies textbooks published today state in the preface and in the teacher's manual that it is necessary for the child to unlearn his old values; he comes to school "damaged by the concepts he has received during the first five years of life, and requires mental healing."—Representative John R. Rarick of Louisiana in a reprint distributed by The Network of Patriotic Letter Writers[1]

Now the public school is making a frontal attack on Protestant ethics. And they [*sic*] make their attack by using our children; the young are grist for their mills, and the young come from us. They use our children to form a secular-humanist America.—from "A Christian Mother's View of the Values Clarification Program"[2]

In light of the ban on prayer in public schools, it is incredible that the principles of Godless Secular Humanism have become the basis for much of public education. To committed Christians and those who

amount of time to carry those out. I feel that I am being dismissed for reasons other than my teaching performance.[26]

Jackie Zykan, a parent of a high school junior, strongly agrees with Mrs. DuPont. "JoAnn was secretary of the Warsaw Community Education Association, and that was a strike against her even though she is an outstanding teacher. She ran her business classes like an office. And some of those kids were in there for two and three hours. So of course they ate candy and drank pop at their desks. They could do that in business. That's not why JoAnn was fired. She was fired for being an outspoken teacher and an officer of the WCEA."

Anne Summe is another person disturbed by the dismissal of Ms. Burnau and Mrs. DuPont and the resignation of three other high school teachers. Ms. Summe was editor of the student newspaper during the 1977–78 school year. She wrote an editorial expressing her dismay at the dismissals and forced resignations. She wrote that she felt as if "I am in the middle of World War III. This school is lying flat on its back, and if it is ever going to get back on its feet again, a peace treaty is going to have to be signed. Otherwise, we might as well forget this school we call ours, and let it turn into just another second-rate school."[27] After Principal Smith told Ms. Summe that she could not publish the editorial, she called the Student Press Law Center in Washington, D.C. Advised of her constitutional rights under the First Amendment, Ms. Summe told Mr. Smith that she would appeal his decision to the school board. He permitted publication of the editorial.

Shortly after the new principal of the high school began work in August, 1978, he called Anne Summe and her parents into his office. He told Ms. Summe that she was "part of a problem" and requested that she sign a document stating that she would not participate on the staff of the newspaper. The principal also indicated that the newspaper might not be funded because of "problems" in the past. Ms. Summe refused to sign the letter of resignation. *KONTAC* had not been published by January of 1979. The student reporters have been told that they

9

can publish school news in the *Times-Union*. A law suit has been filed in federal court on behalf of the students.

Ms. Summe's editorial and Ms. Burnau's choices of books were not the only materials found to be objectionable during the 1977–78 school year. Even before the school year began, the school board indicated, by approval of the following policy in a special session on June 20, that it did not hold academic freedom in high regard: "Any multi-page teacher-made material used as a source of instruction must have prior approval by the principal and the superintendent and be printed at the Instructional Materials Center before it can be formally utilized in the classroom. This excludes review sheets and teacher-made tests."[28]

These two sentences were included in the minutes of the meeting of the school board on October 10: ". . . Dr. Bragg states there are some books in question at this time. He states a directive was issued to principals in the third week of August asking them to respond to him about any books that were in poor taste, and that responses have been received."[29] On October 18, Principal Smith sent a memo that included this directive to all teachers in the high school: "Any classroom materials that you have in your room that might be objectionable, please bring them to the office."[30]

Responding to that directive, Arleen Miner showed Mr. Smith portions of a literature textbook that she had used for at least three years. She pointed to a few words such as *damn* and *hell* and asked if they were now considered objectionable. When Mr. Smith replied, "Yes," Mrs. Miner asked if the words should be blacked out so that the seniors in her class could not read them. Mr. Smith apparently tried to do so and discovered that the ink bled through to the other side of the page. When Mrs. Miner asked if she should remove the "objectionable" pages, he told her to do so. She collected the books from the seniors, and visibly trembling, cut four pages from each copy of the text. Mrs. Miner later said that the offensive story, "A Chip Off the Old Block," had never caused problems before Mr. Smith's directive to remove all "objectionable" material from the classroom.

On January 9, 1978, Mr. Chapel read the following resolution during the meeting of the school board, and it was passed

10

unanimously: "Be it resolved the teachers, administrators and staff of this school district shall be directed to teach students to avoid the use of profanity and obscenities, also books and materials that could be construed as objectionable in this community shall not be used."[31]

Five days before the passage of the Chapel resolution, the president of the Warsaw Community Education Association (WCEA) filed a complaint with the Indiana Education Employment Relations Board, alleging the commission of unfair labor practices. The complaint cited eleven alleged infractions committed by the school board. The complaint was considered to be by far the largest and most complex unfair labor practice grievance filed by teachers in Indiana. The eleven charges against the school board included its:

1. unilaterally changing the personal leave policy without discussing this change.

2. unilaterally changing the curriculum of the Washington Elementary School.

3. unilaterally and forcibly transferring four teachers from Washington Elementary School to another school.

4. unilaterally banning an English textbook.

5. unilaterally changing the high school English curriculum.

6. unilaterally changing the length of lunch periods on non-student attendance days.

7. by-passing the exclusive representative, WCEA, on the matter of non-student attendance days.

8. unilaterally changing working conditions for English and home economics teachers.

9. unilaterally changing working conditions for Leesburg Elementary School teachers by establishing a check-in system.

10. unilaterally changing working conditions for employees by adopting other check-in systems.

11. having high school principal, C. J. Smith, unilaterally administer an arbitrary and capricious textbook censorship program.[32]

11

About three weeks after the WCEA filed the complaint against the school board, the *Times-Union* published an editorial under the headline, "Frivolous Charges." The editorial writer noted: "On the face of them, the alleged infractions would be termed by a court of law as frivolous, irresponsible, costly, and inflammatory. However, collective bargain [*sic*] laws are loaded on behalf of unions, so the designated school authorities may not be able to get a fair shake in an unfair labor practices hearing, which can only further disrupt the educational processes of the Warsaw Community School Corp."[33] That editorial was accompanied by an editorial cartoon depicting a female teacher arguing nose to nose with a member of the school board. The teacher is shouting "Unfair!" The school board member replies, "Just Common Sense!" Peeking out at the reader between the two adversaries is a bewildered child. The cartoon is labeled "Very Taxing!"

The editorial and editorial cartoon reflected the newspaper's attitude toward the teachers. Prior to, as well as during, the four day unfair labor practice hearing in the summer of 1978, the newspaper published a series of editorial cartoons, letters to the editor, and full page advertisements that left no doubt as to where it stood regarding the teachers, the banned books, and the hearing officer who conducted the unfair labor practice hearing.

During the meeting of the school board that was conducted thirteen days before the unfair labor practice hearing began, Carl Davis, a school patron, read excerpts from *Go Ask Alice* in "embarrassed silence." According to the *Times-Union,* Mr. Davis said that he and others were at the board meeting to support the banning of the book "and to ask the board to please protect our children from such material."[34] Jack Lowry, a patron who accompanied Mr. Davis, told the school board that there's "absolutely no educational value in that text or in the two or three others banned." Anthony Zykan, another patron, told the board that he would not presume to "read the *Bible* out of context and I wouldn't presume to comment on that book out of context."[35] The *Times-Union* printed the news story containing the excerpts from *Go Ask Alice* on page three. On page one,

the newspaper printed a cautionary note: "A school parent reads explicit words from a controversial textbook removed from Warsaw Community High School, and some readers may find the excerpts objectionable. Reader discretion is advised."[36]

The next day William K. Mollenhour, editorial editor of the *Times-Union,* initialed an editorial entitled "Filthy Language." In it he apologized "to any reader who was offended by the dirty, filthy and vulgar language." He added: "It was language taken verbatim from a textbook to which students in our school system had already been exposed."[37] He pointed out that some patrons and some reporters from outside newspapers complained about book bannings in Warsaw. Mr. Mollenhour concluded: "Again, The Times-Union regrets the necessity of re-printing the objectionable words of the textbook in order that the public would recognize the charges of censorship and stifling academic freedom for what they are—pure garbage."

Five days before the hearing, the *Times-Union* reported that Carl Davis and Sharon Lowry had formed "People Who Care," an organization that "seeks to rally support for the beleaguered school board and heighten public awareness about the issues at stake in the community's educational system."[38] "People Who Care" ran a full page advertisement in the newspaper, asking parents to cut out a coupon and mail it to the organization. The message on the coupon follows: "Yes! I wish to express my support for the present school board in removing textbooks containing filthy, vulgar language, in switching from immoral libertine courses to basics and instituting honest teacher evaluation!"[39] The advertisement contained a picture of the cover of *Go Ask Alice* with this copy under it: " 'Go Ask Alice' is only one among several text books the School Board has removed from the High School curriculum. The teachers insist on using questionable text books for our children . . . under the guise of instruction . . . in English literature. . ."[40]

Perhaps the tension in the middle school in which the unfair labor practice hearing was conducted would have been just as great without the full page advertisements, the cartoons, and the editorials. But as I sat there during three days of the hearing, I never relaxed in the charged atmosphere, nor, seemingly,

13

did anyone in the room. The entire issue at the hearing concerned the fact that the teachers charged the administration and the school board with making significant changes in working conditions without first consulting the official bargaining agent of the teachers. Under Indiana statute, working conditions cannot be changed significantly without prior discussion.

In his opening statement, the attorney for the school board noted that the teachers wanted the administration to stop long enough to discuss a few insignificant "snowflakes in a blizzard of decision making." The attorney attempted to discuss the literary merits of the banned books and the problems administrators face when a school has a phase-elective English program. But the hearing examiner would not permit discussion of the books since that was not the focal point of the hearing. As the hearing examiner had to note on several occasions, the hearing dealt specifically with the alleged failure of the school board to discuss working conditions before they were changed. The hearing examiner's insistence that both sides focus only on the issues at hand led the newspaper to publish a cartoon in which the officer was pictured as a hanging judge who did not want to be confused with facts. Three months after the hearing, the examiner submitted his recommendation that the school board be ordered "to reverse all policies" noted in the original complaint "to status quo positions."[41]

The school board announced that it would appeal the hearing examiner's recommendation; however, during November and December of 1978, two members of the school board met with two bargaining officials of the WCEA to affect a compromise. The school board agreed to write letters of explanation to the four transferred Washington teachers, to follow its own textbook review procedures in the future, to discuss possible curriculum changes with teachers before they are made, and to refrain from making major changes in working conditions without consulting the WCEA.

The struggle in Warsaw has not ended. Several teachers believe that the compromise with the school board was a mistake, and they say that teaching conditions have not improved. Relationships between the teachers and the school board and

14

central administration have been strained even more by the filing of four complaints in federal courts. In late winter of 1979, the Indiana State Teachers Association filed complaints against the school board in behalf of Teresa Burnau and JoAnne Du-Pont, charging that the dismissal of the teachers violated their constitutional rights under the First Amendment. During the same time period, the Indiana Civil Liberties Union filed two suits in behalf of students at Warsaw Community High School. The first charges that the school board violated the First Amendment rights of Anne Summe and Jeri Grisso by suspending the student newspaper. The second is a class action suit filed in behalf of Brooke and Blair Zykan, charging that the school board, through a series of actions described in this chapter, violated the right of students in Warsaw to know and to read. The four complaints combined seek answers to these questions:

Do secondary school teachers enjoy academic freedom? Do students have the right to know? If they do, is that right predicated on the teachers' right to teach? Should the sensibilities of school board members serve as the sole guide as to what should be taught in the public schools and what methods should be used? Do school board members have the obligation to read a book in its entirety before acting on it? If a school corporation has a set of procedures for reviewing books that have been challenged by a member of the community, should board members be required to follow the same set of procedures before they ban a book? Do school board members have the right to remove a course from the curriculum simply because they do not like it? Do they have the right to remove a course without examining it thoroughly? Do they have the right to deny students the right to learn about a subject? Do school board members have the right, as occurred in Warsaw, to remove a course based on hearsay objections and ban a book based on the reviews of two unidentified psychologists? (The

reviews were introduced into the board meeting 26 days after the book was ordered destroyed and the course removed from the curriculum.) Can a teacher be dismissed simply for protesting a decision of an administrator? Does a teacher have the right to disagree with an administrator? What is objectionable? Who can decide what is objectionable? If school boards and administrators have the right to remove anything from classrooms that they find objectionable, will there be anything left to teach in some school corporations? Can the term *objectionable* be used to intimidate a teacher to the extent that the individual would use scissors to remove pages from a textbook that contained a few *hells* and *damns*? Do student editors and reporters enjoy specific privileges accorded them by the First Amendment?

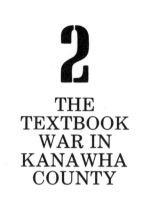

THE
TEXTBOOK
WAR IN
KANAWHA
COUNTY

West Virginia's Kanawha County captured the attention of millions of newspaper readers with its textbook controversy in 1974. Many Americans were obviously shocked when they read that a series of disputes over textbooks led to schools being dynamited, people being shot, and coal mines being closed down. Those tragedies were only part of "the battle of the books"[1] that John Egerton, a free-lance writer, called "in part a class war, a cultural war, a religious war. It is a struggle for power and authority that has sundered a peaceful community into rigid and fearful factions. And it is a complex and profoundly disturbing reflection of the deep fissures that crisscross American society."[2]

Citizens of Warsaw might think that the writer was describing their textbook conflict instead of the one in Charleston, West Virginia; for, with the exception of the violence in Kanawha County, both disputes have much in common. Each struggle was precipitated by a member or members of the school board. Each battle fire was fanned by outside agents or agencies that supplied reviews of textbooks, tactical advice, and other infor-

17

mation. Each conflict had its opponents and proponents of academic freedom. Each dispute led to the formation of a local group or groups of concerned citizens against textbooks. Each confrontation left deep battle scars in the community. And both battles were so complex that they defied superficial analysis.

The Kanawha County war began on March 12, 1974, but the first shot was not fired until April 11. During the March meeting of the school board, the five-member teacher committee submitted a list of 325 English language arts textbooks for approval. Working with teacher subcommittees, the textbook selection committee screened the books on the lists approved by the State of West Virginia. After examining the state-approved texts, the local committee recommended books for use in Kanawha County and submitted the list to the school board for approval.[3] According to Franklin Parker, a professor of education at West Virginia University, the "county's diverse students and school programs were factors in text selection. High schools needed a large number of supplementary texts to meet both the multicultural and multi-ethnic mandate of the 1970 state law and students' varied reading and learning needs."[4]

Alice Moore, a member of the school board, missed the March meeting, but she did attend the meeting in April in which the school board "voted unanimously to adopt the texts but to delay purchase until they could be studied more thoroughly."[5] Mrs. Moore made the motion to delay purchase of the texts.

According to James C. Hefley in *Textbooks on Trial,*[6] Mrs. Moore had made several telephone calls to Mr. and Mrs. Mel Gabler, founders of Educational Research Analysts in Longview, Texas. (See chap. 8.) Mrs. Moore asked the Gablers to send her reviews of the books approved by the teacher selection committee.

Mrs. Moore contended that "most of the books on the language arts list contained material that was disrespectful of authority and religion, destructive of social and cultural values, obscene, pornographic, unpatriotic, or in violation of individual and familial rights of privacy."[7] She noted: "I know that state law says our books must reflect multiracial, multiethnic and multicultural viewpoints, but that's no excuse for teaching or

18

even legitimizing nonstandard English, for example. Or for including book selections that paint Christianity in a bad or hypocritical light." Mrs. Moore said that if schools "can't remain neutral on religion, textbooks should make no mention of it at all."[8]

Appearing at a special meeting of the school board on May 16, the textbook selection committee "explained how the recommended texts would advance the language arts program. Mrs. Moore interrupted, challenging the philosophy of the language arts program and the content of some books."[9]

The wife of a self-ordained minister,[10] Mrs. Moore launched a vigorous campaign against the textbooks in the fundamentalist churches in Kanawha County. The battlelines were drawn. On June 24, "ten ministers gave support to the books; on June 26 twenty-seven opposing ministers called the books immoral and indecent."[11] Nearly a thousand people attended the June 27 meeting of the school board, which voted three to two to drop eight of the most widely criticized books and to keep the rest.[12] That action did not satisfy the textbook protesters who continued making statements about the books throughout the summer. Several ministers proposed "private fundamentalist schools"[13] as one answer for parents who did not want their children to study the objectionable books.

Some of the protesters found books objectionable if they contained the works of controversial black writers like Eldridge Cleaver and Gwendolyn Brooks.[14] Others objected to books that described violence, contained dirty words, or were depressing. Some protesters even objected to an illustrated version of *Jack and the Beanstalk* "because it teaches children to kill and to steal."[15]

Like nine other ministers in the county, the Reverend James Lewis supported the books. "The books in question are creative books," he said, "written with the intention of helping our children discover the truths. Using selections from Winston Churchill to the writer of Ecclesiastes, from Wordsworth to Bernard Malamud, from Richard Brautigan and Kurt Vonnegut to Richard Wright and Elizabeth Browning, these books open up a world of opinion and insight. They're not un-American

or ungodly." But the Reverend Lewis added that he felt the county was "experiencing a religious crusade as fierce as any out of the Middle Ages. Our children are being sacrificed because of the fanatical zeal of our fundamentalist brothers who claim to be hearing the deep, resonant voice of God."[16]

During the first week of school, the textbook protesters kept eight thousand students home from school, and more than four thousand miners stayed off their jobs to show their displeasure with the books. Pickets closed bus depots, grocery stores, and construction sites. They also closed the board of education building in Charleston, which had several of its windows blown out by shotgun blasts.

Like it or not, the residents of Kanawha County discovered that the daily skirmishes in their textbook war made headlines in newspapers from coast to coast. During the turbulent month of September, these incidents and others, were reported:

SEPTEMBER 8. One of the textbook protesters "waved a red sixth grade textbook at the gathering. 'This is the first step of communism,' she said. . . . By week's end, demonstrators had crippled some of the county's industry with picket lines."[17]

SEPTEMBER 11. The school board announced that all of the adopted textbooks would be submitted for review by a citizens' committee. The school board also decided to remove two textbook series and all supplementary texts from classrooms during the review period.[18]

SEPTEMBER 12. "Students at George Washington High School walked out today at 11 a.m. in protest of the decision by the Kanawha County Board of Education to remove controversial English textbooks from schools for a 30-day review period." A spokesman for the students said they saw nothing wrong with the books and that they wanted them back in the classrooms. He also said, "We felt it's hard to let a minority rule the majority."[19]

20

SEPTEMBER 14. As a result of the textbook protest, a truck driver was shot and wounded. The sheriff of Kanawha County said his deputies needed help to control the bands of roving pickets who were shouting, "Burn those filthy books!" Another man was wounded at a picket line, and Superintendent Kenneth Underwood closed the schools and canceled extracurricular activities for the weekend.[20]

SEPTEMBER 15. One man was shot and another was beaten. Both were reported in critical condition.[21] A high school teacher of English said that teachers and administrators "had been threatened repeatedly. We are living again in the climate of a Nazi world," she said. She added that the mob is trying to control everything and direct the lives of everybody.[22] The Kanawha County teachers voted against a one day sick-out to protest the school board's decision to have the adopted textbooks reviewed by a committee of citizens. The teachers felt that the school board's "compromise action was an affront to their profession." However, the teachers feared that the sick-out protest would only "rekindle sparks of violence that appeared to have eased in the valley."[23]

SEPTEMBER 16. Superintendent Underwood announced that the schools will be closed "until I can be assured that students and staff can go to school without fear of violence."[24]

SEPTEMBER 17. Superintendent Underwood decided to reopen the schools after "community and law enforcement officials convinced him it would be safe."[25]

SEPTEMBER 19. Three ministers were among the eleven men arrested for violating a court injunction limiting the number of pickets allowed to congregate on county school property.[26]

SEPTEMBER 23. Alice Moore said that she would not appoint representatives to the citizens' review committee because "it is stacked against those who find some of the current

textbooks offensive." She added that instead of voting on the books, the committee should establish firm guidelines and examine each textbook in light of the guidelines. "The basic guideline should be that the books contain no material which is offensive to any ethnic or cultural group."[27]

SEPTEMBER 27. The Reverend Ezra Graley said that a list of demands would be presented to Kanawha County officials. The demands included: (1) the resignation of Superintendent Underwood and three school board members; (2) removal of all controversial books from county schools; (3) a review of other books in the system by a committee of seven—four to be appointed by the protesters and three by the school board; (4) a "public commitment by the governor to investigate the selection and qualifications of the state textbook committee"; (5) "immediate exoneration of persons accused or convicted of violations of court injunctions during the text controversy"; (6) no job penalties other than loss of wages for textbook protesters who stayed off their jobs; (7) no penalties to students whose parents "cooperated with the textbook protest group."[28]

SEPTEMBER 30. The Reverend Charles Quigley made a statement in which he asked for prayers for the death of three school board members who supported the adoption of the textbooks. "I am asking Christian people to pray that God will kill the giants that have mocked and made fun of dumb fundamentalists."[29]

Violence continued throughout October and November. "Sixteen persons, including a minister, were arrested as they tried to keep school buses at nearby St. Albans from leaving a garage."[30] Eleven mines were shut down and school buses were vandalized.[31] Three gasoline-filled beer bottles were thrown at Chandler Elementary School.[32] A car belonging to one of three women arrested for picketing was destroyed in an explosion.[33] Two school buses were struck by shotgun blasts, and a car belonging to parents who sent their children to school during the protest was fire bombed.[34] "A state police car escorting a

school bus loaded with children was struck by sniper fire."[35]

Early in October, Alice Moore invited Mr. and Mrs. Mel Gabler to fly to Charleston for "a whirlwind six-day speaking campaign." Both spoke at a city-wide rally on their first day in Charleston; then they separated and each was "chauffered up and down the valley . . . speaking twice daily to groups of concerned parents."[36] The Gablers had already sent Mrs. Moore reviews of the textbooks the teacher selection committee had submitted to the school board for approval. And the Gablers also gave Mrs. Moore a copy of the Texas state textbook adoption guidelines,[37] which Mrs. Moore was able to use most effectively.

On November 21, 1974, the Board of Education of Kanawha County adopted these seven textbook guidelines:

I. Textbooks for use in the classrooms of Kanawha County shall recognize the sanctity of the home and emphasize its importance as the basic unit of American society.

Textbooks must not intrude into the privacy of students' homes by asking personal questions about inner feelings or behavior of themselves or their parents, or encourage them to criticize their parents by direct questions, statements or inferences.

II. Textbooks must not contain profanity.

III. Textbooks must respect the right of ethnic, religious or racial groups to their values and practices and not ridicule those values or practices.

IV. Textbooks must not encourage or promote racial hatred.

V. Textbooks must encourage loyalty to the United States and the several states and emphasize the responsibilities of citizenship and the obligation to redress grievances through legal processes.

VI. Textbooks shall teach the true history and heritage of the United States and of any other countries studied in the curriculum. Textbooks must not defame our nation's founders or misrepresent the ideals and causes for which they struggled and sacrificed.

VII. Textbooks used in the study of the English language shall teach that traditional rules of grammar are a worthwhile subject for academic pursuit and are essential for effective communication among English speaking people.[38]

Responding to a request from the Kanawha County Association of Classroom Teachers, the National Education Association sent an inquiry panel into Charleston to conduct a thorough investigation of the textbook controversy. In its published report,[39] the panel commented on the possible effect of the textbook guidelines on education in Kanawha County. The comments bear repeating here:

The first of these guidelines—requiring textbooks to recognize the sanctity of the home—conveys a value that the Board of Education has directed the schools to impart. It is an admirable value, although some very admirable writings—including some of the writings of Shakespeare and Dickens, and some portions of the Holy Bible—if taken out of context, might fail to meet this criterion.

There is, in fact, not one of the adopted guidelines that is value-free. Nor can there be any literature that is value-free, for literature contains ideas; and ideas concern values. The only way in which a school system could approach neutrality would be to offer students a random multiplicity of literature and ideas and

24

values, and permit them to select and read randomly with no guidance from teachers; and no one is proposing this. It must be assumed then that the anti-text leaders in Kanawha County are equating a "neutral" education with an education that is simply non-controversial, according to their own values and traditions.

If the recently adopted guidelines were interpreted in the way that the Textbook Review Committee Splinter Group appears to have interpreted them in its review of the disputed texts, the enforcement of the guidelines would impose upon the public schools the task of indoctrinating students to one system of cultural and religious values, inflexible and unexamined.

Retention of the guidelines could prohibit future history texts from telling the true story of Watergate because that story might cause some students to question the superiority of our government to all others; and it would surely, if told truly, contain profanity. Enforcement of these criteria could prevent history books from telling the true story of the black experience in this country, or of how the west was won, because those stories might offend the dominant race in this nation, might defame the nation's founders, and might induce students to question the opportunity that the nation has provided for the redress of grievances through legal processes. The guidelines would undoubtedly exclude from any future textbook the history of the present controversy in Kanawha County. Such a history, if truly told, would contain profanity and it would perhaps encourage racial hatred. If told from the viewpoint of the text opponents, it would clearly violate the guidelines concerning the "obligation to redress grievances through legal processes."

25

In short, the enforcement of these guidelines, as they are likely to be interpreted by their proponents, would destroy education in the Kanawha County Public Schools.

In addition to adopting the textbook guidelines, the Board of Education of Kanawha County approved a new set of textbook adoption procedures that called for the appointment of a screening committee by the school board. Under the procedures, each board member will appoint three parents and one teacher to a screening committee for each subject area. "This screening committee—composed of 75% parents and 25% teachers—shall examine all books submitted by publishers for the purpose of eliminating those textbooks and related materials that do not meet the Board of Education guidelines—as those guidelines are interpreted by the committee. A 75% vote will be required to eliminate any textbook."[40] Two months after approving the procedures, "the Board of Education revised this decision to provide that a 75% vote will be required to *retain* any textbook."[41]

Thus the textbook protesters in Kanawha County scored two major victories even though they did not succeed in eliminating all of the textbooks. However, according to the National Education Association, the new set of textbook adoption procedures would virtually guarantee that the textbook protesters would be able to impose their concept of education on the entire county. The Inquiry Panel of the NEA wrote: "There are many aspects of the textbook adoption procedures that will make the selection and adoption of instructional materials a nearly impossible task—and a nightmare. The process can only founder amidst a welter of committees, teams, and councils that have been created. Under the new system, the influence of lay citizens is not only present; it literally permeates every area of curriculum planning and textbook evaluation. The screening committees, a curriculum advisory council, preliminary curriculum committees, and curriculum study teams all contain parents as well as teachers. The textbook selection committee alone is composed solely of professional educators. But by the

time this committee begins to function, the range of materials left to select from may have been so narrowed as to make a mockery of the selection process."[42]

The NEA Inquiry Panel also noted that the textbook adoption procedures "will make censors of parents, will constitute an abdication of the Board's legal obligation to maintain responsible control of the schools, and will endanger—if not destroy—the atmosphere of free inquiry and the free exchange of ideas without which education cannot survive."[43]

On November 8, 1974, the school board voted four to one to return all of the controversial textbooks to the schools with the exception of the D.C. Heath *Communicating* series for grades one through six and level four of Houghton Mifflin's *Interaction* series. The two series were placed in school libraries and could be used as supplementary reading with parental approval.[44] Superintendent Underwood resigned his position, and the new superintendent asked the school board to return all books to the classroom, which the board did by a vote of four to one, calling for parental consent for the use of the most controversial books.[45]

Four years after the textbook war, Alice Moore commented: "I see no way to ultimately salvage the public school system. We must fight for what we can while it lasts for the sake of the children who are trapped in it and pray for those good teachers and educators who are still there." She added that concerned parents must also fight for a federal tax credit that will allow them to choose private schools for their children. She said the tax credit would force public schools to improve to meet the private school competition or close completely. "Isn't this what the American way is all about?" she asked.[46]

Reporters, educators, scholars, religious leaders, parents, and free-lance writers have written about the battle of the books in Kanawha County. Many tried to determine the causes of the conflict and provide strategies that might prevent future battles. But most of the writers agreed that there were no easy solutions. For, as Superintendent Underwood noted, "It might take a decade before we can understand what happened."[47]

BOOK
BATTLES
WEST OF THE
MISSISSIPPI
RIVER

"Censorship can never happen here. This city's too sophisticated for that."

"Small towns—not big cities—have censorship problems."

"Only conservative backwaters breed censorship."

Statements like those have been uttered by teachers, librarians, and school administrators in hundreds of communities. And the speakers believe what they are saying—at least until they experience a censorship attack. Once they have become targets of the censors, the victims realize that censorship can—and does—happen anywhere. No community is immune. No city is too large or too sophisticated to escape the censors; no town is too small or too insulated to be protected. To the people who attempt to censor school materials, there are no geographical boundaries. And a successful attempt to censor a specific book in

a city or town on one coast may spur a group on the other coast or in the Ohio valley to try to remove the same book from the local schools.

Since the battle of the books in Kanawha County in 1974, incidents of censorship or attempts at censorship have increased markedly. During the 1977–78 school year, more incidents of removing or censoring books occurred nationally than at any other time in the last twenty-five years.[1] Judith F. Krug, director of the Office for Intellectual Freedom of the American Library Association, told a reporter that roughly three hundred book banning or censorship incidents were reported to her office during 1977–78. Of that number, she estimated that ninety per cent involved schools.[2] In 1976, fewer than two hundred censorship incidents were reported to her office. What upsets the censors? How do they operate? How successful are they? Those questions can be partially answered by examining a series of censorship incidents from coast to coast. With the exception of the book burning in Drake, North Dakota, the incidents reported here have all occurred since the textbook controversy in Kanawha County.

ANAHEIM, CALIFORNIA. When teachers of English in Anaheim's junior and senior high schools were asked to provide the administration and the school board with lists of books they would like to teach, they did not think that they were drawing up a restricted list for the school board, which told the teachers they could use only the 270 books on it.[3] One veteran teacher learned that she could no longer use the paperbacks that had been part of her tenth and eleventh grade courses for nearly ten years. The teacher had to store dozens of books that she had accumulated and had assigned as supplementary reading for the students in her literature classes. Into the boxes to be stored went copies of John Steinbeck's *East of Eden,* Richard Wright's *Black Boy,* and Catherine Marshall's *Christy,* among others.[4]

"Most of the teachers who participated in the revision of the curriculum did not realize those books not on the new list would not be available for supplemental reading," the English teacher said. But the president of the Anaheim Board of Education

29

disagreed with her. "The only effort to restrict comes from the content of basic grammar classes," he said. "If they teach grammar properly, they will have no need for further books. Nor will they have time for them."[5]

The teachers of Anaheim had been touted locally for designing a program that strives to emphasize the basics of grammar. But their attempt to get in step with the back-to-basics movement was not intended to lead to the crating of all of Shakespeare but *Hamlet* and *Romeo and Juliet* and all of Dickens except *Oliver Twist*.[6] The teachers claim they were told that they might mention books other than those on the list of 270 acceptable titles but that they "may not open the books or discuss their content with students." The teachers maintain they were told that they would be reprimanded or possibly dismissed if they were caught teaching any of the banned books.[7]

ANDERSON, CALIFORNIA. Students at Anderson Union High School can no longer find Richard Brautigan's poetry and fiction in their library or in their developmental reading classes. The Anderson High principal removed seven Brautigan books in January of 1978, and the school board later voted to ban these five: *The Abortion: An Historical Romance, Trout Fishing in America, The Pill Versus the Springhill Mine Disaster, Rommel Drives on Deep into Egypt,* and *A Confederate General from Big Sur.* The two Brautigan works not banned are *Revenge of the Lawn* and *In Watermelon Sugar.*

According to a complaint filed in the Superior Court of the State of California in and for the County of Shasta,[8] the principal removed the seven Brautigan works from the developmental reading classroom of a teacher who had taught at Anderson High for eight years. The only reason given for removal of the books was that they "are objectionable." The teacher maintained that more than three hundred students have read some or all of Brautigan's works during the eight years he has taught the class and that no student or parent ever objected to any of the books. The principal gave the books to two separate committees for review. One committee reported to the school that three of the Brautigan books "contained definite and explicit material

which the general public would deem unsuitable for children." The committee recommended that "public funding should not be utilized in providing these books to the general student body at Anderson Union High School."[9] Similar recommendations were later made for two more books.

Two teachers of developmental reading, three high school students, and the publisher of Brautigan's works filed suit against the principal and the school board near the end of 1978. The suit calls for the issuance of a judicial declaration that in banning the five books the defendants "acted arbitrarily, capriciously and without justification and in violation of the rights of the plaintiffs as guaranteed" by the California Constitution and by the First and Fourteenth Amendments to the United States Constitution.[10] The suit also calls for a preliminary injunction enjoining the defendants from banning the books from the library and from the curriculum.

CULVER CITY, CALIFORNIA. A group that called itself American Christians in Education protested the adoption of a textbook entitled *Literature of the Supernatural* for an elective course at Culver City Junior High School. Carrying signs with such messages as "Junior High Becoming a Charles Manson Preschool" and "Occult Is Out," approximately ninety pickets marched peacefully in front of the school on a September day in 1976.[11] A leader of the protesting group said that the course was not being taught objectively. "It is only presenting the occultic side of the supernatural and not the theistic side; therefore, this course is indoctrinating and not educating the students."[12]

The Culver City Board of Education carefully considered the book and the course. Each member of the school board read the book, and the board also gave the book to a review committee for examination. The review voted four to one to retain the book and the course; the school board voted three to one to retain both.[13]

In a letter to an editor of a daily newspaper, the Culver City Board of Education noted that the book under question is an anthology in which most of the stories "are classics of literature by authors such as Poe, Bradbury, Lovecraft, O'Henry, H. G.

Wells, Charles McKay, and others."[14] The school board added that upon receipt "of a written protest, we immediately initiated our policy, which is designed to offer us a complete, open, and careful analysis of the protest and the instructional materials in question. Our five-person committee, which we believe to be well qualified and representative, studied the material, met personally with the protesters to hear directly their points of view, deliberated over four meetings, and carefully examined teachers' specific lesson plans for utilization of the materials." The school board wrote: "A disservice is being done to our capable staff by statements or allegations that they will 'teach the occult', etc. You may not be aware we have been offering 'Bible as Literature' as an elective for the past five or six years. *We do not teach and have not taught* religion, nor is our staff, in our opinion, interested in the indoctrination of students."[15]

OAKLAND, CALIFORNIA. A largely autobiographical novel about the life of a twelve year old black girl growing up in a rat infested tenement in Harlem angered a black father when his teenage daughter brought the book home from a junior high school library. The father did not think that Louise Meriwether's widely acclaimed *Daddy Was a Numbers Runner* should be accessible to teenagers.[16] A member of a special panel appointed to review the book said: "I want to underscore that the father has the right to tell his daughter she can't read that. But no one has the right to say 'I'm going to set standards inside the house and outside as well.'"[17]

Appointed by the superintendent to examine the protested book, the review panel found it to be "an honest autobiographical portrait" which presented "an accurate picture of the times." The committee noted that the book "has a great deal of educational merit" and stated that its "occasionally profane language and fairly explicit sex scenes are an important part of the work."[18] The superintendent examined the review panel's report but decided to remove the book from the junior high school library and place it on a highly restricted library shelf in the high school. A former national director of the Right to Read program, the superintendent said that although she does not

"advocate censoring material, I do feel that the public schools have a responsibility to make decisions relative to appropriate reading material."[19] Local, state, and national organizations of teachers and librarians protested the superintendent's decision to remove the book from the library, but she refused to reinstate it.

MILTON-FREEWATER, OREGON. An Oregon court ordered school officials in the Milton-Freewater school district to replace textbooks that had been expurgated. A principal had clipped pages on evolution from the textbooks because they presented evolutionary theory as fact. Two parents of children in the school system filed suit, charging that the removal of the pages of the text violated the First Amendment rights of their children. The attorney for the parents said: "Certainly no one is questioning the right of the Milton-Freewater school district to select textbooks for use in their schools. However, once selected and in use, these books are not subject to the censorship of any person or group, including teachers, principals, superintendents or the board of directors of the school district. Tearing out the material on evolution in a state-approved textbook is unconstitutional censorship."[20]

PORTLAND, OREGON. With the assistance of the American Civil Liberties Union of Oregon, parents of pupils in the Portland and Gresham grade school districts have filed a complaint in the United States District Court for the District of Oregon against members of the Oregon State Board of Education and members of the Oregon State Textbook Commission. The parents contend that an Oregon statute regulating the content of textbooks used in the public schools violates the First and Fourteenth Amendments to the United States Constitution. The contested portion of the statute reads as follows: *Textbooks on American history and government.* Every board, commission, committee or officer responsible for the selection of textbooks for use in the public schools shall select textbooks on American history and government which adequately stress the services rendered by those who achieved our national independence, who established our

form of constitutional government and who preserved our federal union. No textbook shall be used in the schools which speaks slightingly of the founders of the republic or of those who preserved the union or which belittles or undervalues their work.[21]

Filed in November of 1978, the complaint maintains that the statute violates the constitutional rights of the pupils in the following ways:

1. It precludes their learning through their textbooks facts, ideas, and opinions that deviate from those prescribed by the state.

2. It requires that all textbooks on American history and government express a prescribed "patriotic" view of the founders of the country and of those who preserved the federal union.

3. Its vague language deters the exercise of protected speech and thus infringes upon the right of free access to facts, ideas, opinions, and other forms of expression.

4. It is overbroad in that its prohibition encompasses expression which is protected and which the state has no legitimate interest in regulating.

5. It imposes unjustifiable prior restraint on the rights of free expression and of free access to expression.

6. It discourages textbook publishers and distributors from offering to Oregon public schools textbooks which contain proscribed expression and textbooks which lack prescribed expression.[22]

KENT, WASHINGTON. The school board in this Seattle suburb decided to assign sex education duties to school nurses after parents complained about films that fifth graders saw. The parents said that *Growing Into Womanhood* and *Growing Into Manhood* were too explicit in their descriptions of masturbation and of the body's erogenous zones. The school superintendent said he doubted that the films will be used in the future. Parents did have the opportunity to preview the films before they were used in the classes, but few took advantage of the opportunity.[23]

ISSAQUAH, WASHINGTON. Shortly after the school board voted to ban J. D. Salinger's *The Catcher in the Rye* from high school classrooms, the people of Issaquah recalled the three school board members who voted against the book. In addition to their voting against the book, several other actions of the three school board members precipitated the recall vote. The trio had voted to transfer a part of the school district to another district, and they also voted not to renew the contract of the superintendent[24] who had strongly defended the use of *The Catcher* in English classes.

The woman who spearheaded the drive to oust *The Catcher* told the school board that she had counted 785 "profanities" in the book. "When a book has 222 'hells,' 27 'Chrissakes,' seven 'hornys,' . . . then it shouldn't be in our public schools," she said. She also stated that the teaching of the book brainwashes students and is "part of an overall Communist plot in which a lot of people are used and may not even be aware of it."[25]

ST. ANTHONY, IDAHO. An English teacher who taught Ken Kesey's *One Flew Over the Cuckoo's Nest* to one of his English classes was placed on probation during his second year of teaching and his contract was not renewed at the end of the year. After several parents complained about the language in the book, the superintendent collected all copies from the students. The superintendent said that he did not try to judge the book in literary terms because he is not a literary critic. "But I am a critic about what's proper in the classroom. I'm an authority on what's proper in the classroom. Because of it's language the book is not proper in the classroom."[26]

But several of the students and the teacher disagreed with the superintendent, who, according to the teacher, removed the book without reading it or taking any steps to determine its literary or scholastic value.[27] The teacher said that he sent parents of the students a list of books to be read in his class. He also said that if a student chose not to read the book, an alternate assignment would be made. No one returned the book.[28] Working with the American Civil Liberties Union, the teacher has filed a complaint in the United States District Court for the

District of Idaho, charging that the administration violated his rights as guaranteed by the First and Fourteenth Amendments, as well as the rights of his students.[29]

THATCHER, ARIZONA. When the librarian of Thatcher High School returned to school in the fall of 1978, she found that "the library had been stripped of virtually all periodicals. In action apparently approved by the school board, more than 1,100 volumes representing back issues of sixty-five titles were removed." She also learned that many subscriptions had been canceled and that back issues of only these magazines could be kept in the library: *Arizona Highways, National Geographic, Newsweek,* and *Time.*

Neither the school board nor the superintendent gave official reasons for the removal of the periodicals. "It was rumored that the board was told that teachers made no assignments involving periodicals. In previous years administrators had complained about 'inappropriate' articles and advertisements. In one incident last year, an issue of *Time* with an article on swimwear fashions was taken from the library and from all students in a current events class."[30]

JACKSON, WYOMING. The Teton County school board voted to remove *Growing Up Female* from the library of Jackson Hole High School. The parent who complained about the book at a public meeting of the school board said that he was shocked by the sexually explicit photographs. He suggested that the school librarian be fired. The school board appointed a review committee from the audience to study the protested book, and the committee not only recommended that it be removed from the library but also suggested the establishment of a committee to review all of the books in the high school.[31]

HELENA, MONTANA. The school board voted seven to three to remove *Our Bodies, Ourselves* from all school libraries in Helena. The decision followed the receipt of a three page letter about the book from an official in the office of the Attorney General of Montana. The official explained that in his opinion a

person "commits the offense of Endangering the Welfare of Children" by "assisting, promoting or encouraging a child to engage in sexual conduct." He added that a librarian who made the book "available to children under the age of sixteen could be subject to criminal charges."[32] The head of the local unit of Phyllis Schlafly's Eagle Forum requested the letter from the Montana official. "In a related development, Eagle Forum members succeeded in placing on the November ballot a measure which would allow Montana municipalities to enact laws on obscenity which would have 'tougher' standards than the state law."[33]

A concerned citizen of Helena, obviously fearing that someone might read the public library's copy of *Our Bodies, Ourselves,* checked out the book in mid-summer and kept it through a series of loan renewals. She said that she regularly checked out "pornographic works" and repeatedly renewed them "to spread the word and keep them off the shelf and out of the hands of children."[34]

DRAKE, NORTH DAKOTA. In addition to the standard textbooks, the English teacher at Drake High School assigned three books: Kurt Vonnegut's *Slaughterhouse Five,* James Dickey's *Deliverance,* and "an anthology of short stories by Ernest Hemingway, Joseph Conrad, John Steinbeck, William Faulkner, and other authors, including numerous Nobel and Pulitzer Prize winners."[35] The school board ordered that all copies of the books should be confiscated and burned. "Although none of the five school board members had read any of the books, they held a meeting, decided that the books were 'dirty' and authorized the book burning."[36]

The burning of *Slaughterhouse Five* attracted so much nationwide publicity that school officials did not have the other two sets of books burned. "I'm not sorry about the action the school board took," the superintendent said. "I don't regret it one bit, and we'd do it again. I'm just sorry about all the publicity that we got. People in Drake are sick and tired of all this publicity."[37]

The English teacher said he "got these books to get the kids

to think clearly about current problems. . . . A few four-letter words in a book is no big deal. These people have all heard these words before; none learned any new words. I've always thought the purpose of school was to prepare these people for living in the 'big, bad world', but it evidently isn't so."[38] The teacher lost his job, but he did win an out-of-court settlement in a suit filed in his behalf by the American Civil Liberties Union. The settlement included these three points: (1) that teachers in the high school may use *Slaughterhouse Five* and *Deliverance* in their junior and senior high school classes, (2) that the teacher's performance at the high school may not be described as unsatisfactory, either orally or in writing, and (3) that the teacher be awarded $5,000.[39]

GARDNER, KANSAS. Copies of Peter Benchley's *Jaws* have been removed from all school libraries in the Gardner-Edgerton-Antioch school district. Responding to a parent who complained about an explicit sexual act in the book, the school board voted unanimously to take the book out of circulation.[40]

EAST BATON ROUGE, LOUISIANA. With the consent of the teachers of the course, the superintendent of the East Baton Rouge school system removed *Mass Media and the Popular Arts* from an elective English course on the news media. The local district attorney admitted that he was interested in the case because a parent had complained about it and because he felt that "the person or persons responsible for presenting the material in the book to persons under 17 would be liable under Louisiana law prohibiting juvenile access to obscene matter."[41] The district attorney said that the allegedly objectionable words in the textbook—terms for sexual intercourse used in articles extracted from periodicals—and two pictures from magazines were, in his opinion, obscene.[42]

Two months later, the school board voted eight to three to keep Isabella Taves's *Not Bad for a Girl* in the elementary school library. The book is about a twelve year old girl's attempt to play on a boys' baseball team. According to a parent who complained about the book's not being appropriate for young

readers, it contains the words *fag, queer, damn* and *damned.*[43]

Six months later, a local author formed an anti-censorship group to "counter the activities of another organization which wants obscene books banned from East Baton Rouge Parish schools." An organization called the Concerned Citizens and Taxpayers for Decent School Books had circulated "a list of books it wants banned, including works by famed authors John Steinbeck and J. D. Salinger as well as an anthropology book, *The Naked Ape.*" The local author said that "the large number of black or Jewish authors make it appear the list is aimed at the race or nationality of the writers." But the Concerned Citizens say they are "against pornography and filth."[44]

The principal of a high school in East Baton Rouge Parish removed Norma Klein's *Sunshine* from a thematic poetry and literature class. The principal said he found the language offensive in a book that tells the "story of a young man and woman who meet and live together. The woman finds she is pregnant by a husband she is separated from. She finds out she has an incurable malignancy. The man and woman eventually marry and he accepts the child as his own. It is based on a true story."[45] The English teacher who assigned the book said that she was aware of one parent's objections to it and that she assigned the student another book, *Death Be Not Proud.*[46]

The East Baton Rouge Parish school board adopted a resolution in mid-September that contained these three sections:

Section 1

The superintendent and his staff shall immediately take all necessary steps to be certain that each school principal and school staff, working cooperatively with the school librarian, devote the proper time and effort to ascertaining whether there are any books and materials containing obscenity, filth, or pornography in their respective schools and that such books or materials be forwarded to the superintendent's office for a fair review and evaluation of each book in question to determine if said book is suitable for use by the children in our school system.

Section 2

The East Baton Rouge Parish School Board again reiterates its total opposition to having any book or other material anywhere in our school system whether as a textbook, available in the school library, or assigned as outside reading which contains any such obscenity, filth, or pornography.

Section 3

The East Baton Rouge Parish School Board again reiterates its welcoming the help of principals, teachers, librarians, parents, and students in bringing to the attention of the proper school authorities any books or material containing obscenity, filth, or pornography.[47]

The leader of the Concerned Citizens group said: "I've got spies in all the schools, pledging to make sure the superintendent does his job."[48]

HOT SPRINGS, ARKANSAS. A father became upset when he discovered that his daughter was reading four-letter words in *Run, Shelley, Run,* a book she had obtained from a junior high school library. The father's complaint about the book resulted in its being "removed and destroyed," according to a school official.[49] "My daughter doesn't need to go to school to learn street language," the father said. "This book deals with four-letter words, drugs, lesbianism, and ineffectual correctional systems, and does it in words that couldn't be printed in the newspaper. The printed word coming out of a school system gives it a stamp of approval."[50]

SPRINGFIELD, MISSOURI. When forty kindergarten children opened copies of Maurice Sendak's *In the Night Kitchen,* they probably didn't even notice that an artist had drawn a pair of shorts over the drawing of a nude boy. The work with a felt-tip pen was commissioned by school officials who thought the altered picture "would be in a little better taste for the community standards."

The director of elementary education said: "Obviously we

40

felt there would be a reaction, so we decided that if the book could be changed without altering it severely, we would do it. We didn't want to detract from the story. We felt it was a good story. I think in the public schools we have to be sensitive to the feelings of people. As far as nudity is concerned I guess I'm an old fogey, but I think it should be covered." Another school official said he felt that the school had not engaged in censorship. "I feel it's a form of using materials that normally wouldn't have been used."[51]

ELKADER, IOWA. The leader of approximately thirty parents who called themselves Concerned Citizens read a two-hour complaint against books used in the Middle School at Volga. The concerned parent contended that the Ginn 360 Reading Series, the Houghton Mifflin Action Series, and *A Piece of the Action* by New Dimensions in Education "contained an undercurrent which definitely undermines our American and Christian principles."[52] The protesting parent included these remarks in her complaint:[53] "Among the writers and those given praise in the reading material are: Ogden Nash, Woodie Guthrie, Langston Hughes, Joan Baez, Gwendolyn Brooks, Malcolm X, and Dick Gregory. These are all known communists or subversive revolutionaries and sympathizers. Hughes, for example, has authored a variety of subversive 'literature', including a blasphemous poem, 'Goodbye Christ' and a piece he calls 'The Workers Song'.

"Fortunately these two pieces are not in our reading material, but they give us insight concerning his motives. Time magazine describes Malcolm X as a 'pimp, cocaine addict and thief' with a creed of violence. The magazine also quotes him, 'If ballots won't work, bullets will.' Dick Gregory, a racial agitator is mentioned with praise in the reading material. This man, not long ago, traveled the country giving obscene speeches and calling our flag 'just another rag', inciting riot and desecration of the American flag."

A careful examination of the text of the concerned parent's reviews of the reading books revealed that much of what she read can be obtained from Educational Research Analysts in Longview, Texas.[54] (See chap. 8.)

The concerned parent also submitted a set of guidelines for textbook selection and recommended that they be approved as part of the new textbook policy.[55] With one exception, the guidelines are identical to those adopted in Kanawha County, West Virginia, which were sent to textbook protesters there by Educational Research Analysts. (See pages 23–24.)

The school board voted six to one to keep the books in the classrooms. The husband of the leader of the Concerned Citizens cast the dissenting vote. The school board received the support of more than eight hundred persons who signed a petition calling for the retention of the books in the curriculum.[56]

BURLINGTON, IOWA. Students at Notre Dame High School in Burlington, Lyons Township High School in LaGrange, Illinois, and Manton Consolidated Schools in Manton, Michigan will no longer be able to read *Car and Driver* in their school libraries. Their school librarians canceled the schools' subscriptions to the magazines to protest an article attacking the federally mandated 55 miles-an-hour speed limit. In response to the letters of cancellation, the editor of the magazine wrote: "What you're telling us is that the book burners are now running the libraries. We thought schools were meant to prepare our youth for real life, not hide it from them."[57]

MONTICELLO, IOWA. The Monticello school board voted four to one to remove *Jack the Bear* from the school library and place it in a "professional library" in the teachers' lounge. The founder of an organization called Concerned Parents opposed the book with the backing of "upwards of 400 people" who told him he was right in objecting to the book. The chairperson of the school board, which ignored the recommendation of a special book review committee to keep the book in the library, said that the board decided against the book because of a four-letter word. "It isn't in every other sentence, but it's pretty heavy," the chairperson said.[58]

WEST DES MOINES, IOWA. All copies of *The Seventeen Gerbils of Class 4a* will be returned to the shelves of the elementary school library, the school superintendent said. He added that the re-

moval of the book was a mistake and that the action occurred while all school board policies, including one for handling challenges to library materials, were being rewritten. The book was erroneously pulled for review after the parents of a second grader complained about the use of the phrase "smartass" in the book. In the future, books will remain on the library shelves during the review process.[59]

BLOOMINGTON, MINNESOTA. An officer of Parents of Minnesota, Inc. filed a complaint with the school board about *Riders on the Earth,* a reading textbook published by Holt, Rinehart and Winston. The complainant charged that the sixth-grade text discriminates against whites, is anti-government, and is "contrary to the Ten Commandments and the laws of the land." Asked to illustrate how the book discriminates against whites, the textbook protester cited a story in which a white adult tells a boy: "I apologize for the stupidity and meanness of my race." The concerned parent said that the book would contribute to the "alienated, confused, cynical, and shiftless" attitudes of youth.[60]

The discovery of three books with "sexually explicit language" in the library of a junior high school "spurred one parent to remove seven of his children from Bloomington schools."[61] The parent said he had been concerned for some time about materials used in the schools, "but when this came out, I really came uncoiled." What disturbed him were Kurt Vonnegut's *Welcome to the Monkey House* and *Again, Dangerous Vision,* a two-volume collection of science fiction stories edited by Harlan Ellison. The Bloomington superintendent said that he "deplores the fact that the obscene books . . . were purchased and made available to students." The books were not ordered through normal channels, the superintendent added. He said that staff members in each school are authorized to buy supplementary materials directly but are "cautioned to use discretion when doing so. We shall take steps to prevent a reoccurence" of the purchase of objectionable material.[62]

EDEN VALLEY, MINNESOTA. After the school board voted to ban Harper Lee's *To Kill a Mockingbird* from high school literature classes, the board reconsidered and voted to reinstate the book

but to remove all copies of *Runaway's Diary* from the schools. A school board member who supported the parents who complained about both books said that *Diary* would be "no help at all to get rid of all the problems we have in school with all the pregnant girls we have each year."

The Minnesota Civil Liberties Union made this statement in a press release: "The school board endorsed certain religious values and thereby mixed church and state in violation of the First Amendment. They also ignored the right of students to learn by exposure to a wide variety of written material, some of which may be offensive to some members of the community. It is the law that books may not be censored merely because they present ideas and lifestyles different from those of parents or members of the community and even despised by them."[63]

FOREST LAKE and ST. ANTHONY–NEW BRIGHTON, MINNESOTA. Since it was first published in the *New Yorker* in 1948, Shirley Jackson's short story, "The Lottery," has been widely acclaimed as a masterpiece. It graphically illustrates the frequent inhumanity of human beings to one another; it also demonstrates the dangers of blindly following superstition and adhering to a cruel tradition. A widely anthologized short story, it has been discussed by hundreds of thousands of students in literature classes throughout the United States. And now it can be seen as well as read. The Encyclopaedia Britannica film has won critical acclaim; it has also incurred the wrath of groups of concerned parents in a number of communities, including both Forest Lake and St. Anthony–New Brighton.

Approximately seventy-five parents in the Forest Lake district claimed that the film portrays "an unrealistic form of tradition" and would cause destruction of the family unit and undermine "values, traditions, and religious beliefs." After a review committee recommended that students in senior English classes be permitted to see the film so long as parents were notified of every showing, the school board voted to bar use of the film because the review committee was a "stacked deck" in favor of the film.[64] Four months later the school board denied the request of a coalition of parents that *The Lottery* be returned to the classroom.[65]

The St. Anthony–New Brighton school district returned the film to the English classroom after a citizen challenged the original review committee's makeup. A new committee was appointed, and it called for use of the film.[66]

PARK RAPIDS, DEER RIVER, and GRAND RAPIDS, MINNESOTA. Groups of concerned citizens in three Minnesota communities charged the schools with being "secular humanistic" (see chap. 7) and demanded the removal of specific books from the curriculum. In two of the three towns, the organizations called themselves Concerned Citizens for a Better Education. Among the targets in the three communities were *Go Ask Alice, Daddy Was a Numbers Runner,* and *Values Clarification.*[67] All three books had been targets of groups of concerned citizens in other communities.

Teachers, administrators, and school board members resisted pressures to remove the books; however, the copy of Louise Meriwether's *Daddy Was a Numbers Runner* was so mutilated that it had to be removed from one school library for that reason.[68] The organizations of concerned parents distributed a number of handouts at meetings in each of the three school districts. Close examination of much of the material revealed that it could be obtained from Educational Research Analysts in Longview, Texas (see chap. 8) as well as from other organizations of concerned parents. In fact, Norma Gabler, cofounder of Educational Research Analysts, spoke to a group of parents in nearby St. Cloud just prior to the local organizations' protests of specific teaching materials.[69]

At a meeting in one of the communities, the leaders of the local organization distributed these "Guidelines for the Selection of School Material":

1. Classroom materials, textbooks, audio and/or visual aids must not portray parents as unloving, stupid, hypocritical, old fashioned, possessive nor in any other negative way.

2. Classroom materials, textbooks, questionaires [*sic*], etc., must respect the privacy of students' homes and must not ask personal questions about inner feelings or behavior of students or of their parents.

45

3. Classroom materials, textbooks, novels, audio and/or visual aids must not contain profanity.

4. Classroom materials, textbooks, novels, audio and/or visual aids must not ridicule the values of any ethnic, religious, or racial group.

5. Classroom materials, textbooks, etc., must not use psycho-drama (role playing) as a teaching tool.

6. Classroom material, textbooks, novels, audio and/or visual aides [*sic*] must not encourage or teach racial hatred. (White or Black)

7. Classroom material, textbooks, novels, audio and/or visual aides [*sic*] must not encourage sedition or revolution against the United States Government or teach that an alien form of government is superior.

8. Classroom material, textbooks, booklets, audio and/or visual aids must not promote pagan culture and life styles.

9. Classroom material and textbooks used in the study of the English language must teach that traditional rules of grammar are a worthwhile subject for academic pursuit and are essential for effective communication.

10. Classroom material, textbooks, booklets, audio and/or visual aids must not defame the nation's historical personalities or misrepresent the ideals and causes for which they struggled and sacrificed.

In other words—textbooks should rather promote the ideals that:

a. Government should only protect the individual against monoply [*sic*], fraud, violence, theft, and physical harm.

b. Government should encourage work productiveness, profit, saving, investment, and individual prosperity.

c. Patriotism or love of country is essential to peace and prosperity in the United States.

d. Biblical teachings of faith, hope, and charity on the part of individuals is [*sic*] essential and should be implied if not dealt with directly.

e. The history of the United States is that of a great

Constitutional Republic, marred in many instances by evil men, but in itself the best system of government yet divised [*sic*].

f. There is a Supreme Power greater than man or nature.

g. The eternal problem of society is to attain the maximum of individual freedom and love of fellow men, with a minimum of government regulation and intervention.

h. Individual responsibility for material well-being, education, happiness and all else is essential to a great society.

i. The family is the basic social unit in our society. Anything that tends to destroy the family is anti-social.

j. Good and evil, self-respect and guilt are necessary for achieving the maximum good and minimum evil in our personal lives.

k. Each is an individual, different from all others except in the eyes of God. In the eyes of God we are equal, regardless of race, color, nationality, wealth or virtue.

l. The United States should cooperate with all countries, but not at the expense of our own national security.

m. Charity and welfare should be given only voluntarily and on an individual basis. Anything else is paternalism and leads eventually to slavery.

n. We can learn to solve the problems of the future from a knowledge of the history of the past related to the present.

o. Intellect without ethical character is potentially dangerous.

Steps to Combat Atheistic Humanism in the Schools
A PLAN OF ACTION

1. Sign and get notarized the "Restriction Notice" to schools.

2. Keep in close contact with your children concerning school work. Question them often (two to three times a week) regarding English, Social Studies, Science, Health

and Home Economics Classes. Check the list on back as to what to look for.

3. Encourage children to bring home objectionable material to be used for showing others. People must see to believe.

4. Call the school principal and teacher every time you find offensive material and COMPLAIN. You are the best judge of what is right for your child.

5. Join or form a committee in your school district, to more effectively combat the Secular Humanism in your school.

6. Contact other parents from your school when you find or hear of something objectionable so they too can complain. *Keep those teachers on their toes. Let them know you are there and WATCHING!*

7. Complain to the School Board members: For those who are unattentive to your concerns, call them at home and complain to them there, choosing a time convenient for you.

8. Tell and show neighbors, friends and relatives what is happening in education so they will understand the situation and be more able to counteract it in their area.

9. Join "Young Parents Alert", a newsletter especially for parents in Minnesota. It will keep you up to date on the school scene and current legislation, etc. Address: P.O. Box 15, Lake Elmo, Mn. 55042. Donations appreciated.

10. Become a member of "Parents of Minnesota, Inc." This is a non-profit organization recently formed to raise money for the sole purpose of defending parental rights and suing the educators responsible for teaching revolutionary concepts in opposition to God, family and country. For membership, send five dollars or more to: Parents of Minnesota, Inc., P.O. Box 118, St. Paul Park, Mn. 55071. OUR FUTURE LIES IN THE COURTS!

11. Work with groups in other school districts. Exchange information with our CITIZENS EDUCATION COMMITTEE: P.O. Box 290, St. Paul Park, Mn. 55071. Have copied objectionable materials that your children bring home as well as review and make a report on offensive portions of books,

magazines, etc. Write the objections, titles, authors, and page number down and share it with us to keep, thereby creating an effective file on school materials and their whereabouts. IMPORTANT! DOCUMENT ALL MATERIAL with name of school, school district, class, grade, and date. *Only by caring and working together can we rid our schools of Atheistic Humanism.*

12. Write to our governor and legislators. Tell them how strongly you feel about the kind of education children are getting. Send them a copy of what you consider objectionable. REMEMBER, SEEING IS BELIEVING.

13. Send for the 40 page booklet "Critical Review" by Mr. Ron Miller and Mrs. Joe Egan. After a great deal of study and some very extensive research, they wrote a report on the objectionable material taught in public schools today, notably Junior Highs. It explains in a clear way how the educators are manipulating our youth with anti-normal attitudes. To be sure, textbooks differ from school to school, but the attitudes promoted are the same everywhere. Write to: Citizens Education Committee, P.O. Box 290, St. Paul Park, Mn. 55071. Enclose 35 cents per copy or 3 copies for $1.00.

We have been endowed by our Creator with certain un-alienable rights over our children and must insist that the schools and legislators recognize and insure those rights.[70]

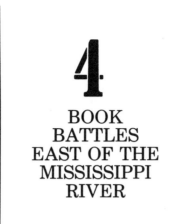

4.

BOOK
BATTLES
EAST OF THE
MISSISSIPPI
RIVER

The attempt by a group of parents to have *Working* removed from the classrooms of Kettle Moraine High School angered Studs Terkel, the author of the best-selling book. When he learned that two hundred parents signed a petition calling for the banning of the book, the author demanded: "How dare they do that! Talk about ignorance and arrogance. How dare they do that, take a thing out of context!"[1] When he heard that the protesting parents objected to the language that a fireman uses in the book, the author was disturbed. "They make this fireman, Tommy Patrick, a dirty man. He's a working fireman, and he's proud of his work because he saves lives. . . In this book he talks with four-letter words they've all heard many times. But mostly he's a wonderful person. He's such a hero."[2]

Working contains interviews with 133 working people in its 762 pages. The author lets the workers tell their own stories in their own words. He interviewed people who worked at all kinds of jobs. He even interviewed a prostitute. And the complaining parents in Wales, a small town near Milwaukee, Wisconsin, disliked the interview with the prostitute and the language the

other workers used. The author said that what the petitioners were trying to do to protect their children is sad. He said that his book is "mostly about the resilience of the human spirit. And to have people attack it as obscene is in itself obscene."[3]

Several of the parents who opposed the book saw a relationship between the "filth of the book," the four-letter words on some desks, and the "drug problem." They blamed the problems on "administrative laxness."[4] One parent was quoted as saying: "It takes only one paragraph to make a book obscene. Therefore, *Working* is obscene because one paragraph contains some ribald, tongue-in-cheek speculations about the possible uses of vaginal sprays."[5] A school board committee recommended that the book be used as supplemental reading and that it not be required of students whose parents objected to it.[6]

ADAMS, WISCONSIN. The school board of the Adams-Friendship School District voted unanimously to remove *Go Ask Alice* from the school library. During the meeting of the board, a parent held up the book, said it was filthy, and offered to read portions of it. The board declined the offer but banned the book.[7]

GREEN BAY, WISCONSIN. A minister told the school board that he and others oppose sex education courses in the schools, and he particularly objected to the use of a film, *Then One Year*, in a sixth-grade class. After thanking the board for removing a behavioral objective from the instructional manual for sixth-grade teachers, the minister protested the film. He said that he was grateful that students would no longer have to write a definition of masturbation, now that the objective had been removed, but he regretted that they had to see the portion of the film dealing with masturbation. He suggested cutting approximately thirty seconds from the film that shows ejaculation.[8]

Backed by a number of residents of Green Bay, the school board voted to keep the film in the curriculum. Before the vote was taken, the board was informed that the film had been shown at a meeting of the Brown County Pastors Association and that "all discussion was positive" by the twenty-five members present.[9]

51

WAUKESHA, WISCONSIN. The Waukesha school board voted not to buy enough copies of two books so that the teacher of a course entitled "Perspectives on Death and Aggression" could assign them to the class as a whole. Copies of Truman Capote's *In Cold Blood* and Glendon Swarthout's *Bless the Beasts and Children* are available to students enrolled in the course, and they will continue to be; however, the board's decision not to purchase more books precludes the entire class from reading and discussing them.[10]

During the heated discussion of the books, one board member said that endorsing the two novels would be "putting a rubber stamp" on violence. She called the Swarthout novel "psychopathically sick," and she added that the mass murder in the Capote novel that is based on fact is "well forgotten."[11] Several members of the board criticized the course, "Perspectives on Death and Aggression," and called for a review of it. After discussing the course with teachers and administrators, board members were apparently satisfied with an "informal review" of the course and the teacher's manual.[12]

WAUZEKA, WISCONSIN. Responding to a protest about Robert Goodman's *Collected Poems,* the Wauzeka school board decided to read the book before taking action on parental requests to have it removed from the library. An attorney who is the husband of a school board member said that only three or four students checked out the book in eight or nine years; therefore, it should not be blamed as the cause of students' foul language or bad conduct. He added: "People ask, as taxpayers, should they be required as taxpayers to pay taxes for this kind of book. You cannot ban books. Banning books leads to banning of other ideas. Free speech is in the law."[13]

One parent noted: "No kid ever knew that book existed until all you people started this. The kids here don't read. If they'll read this, good. Let's put more books like it in (the library)."[14] One month later, the board voted three to two to keep the book in the library.[15]

BRIGHTON, MICHIGAN. The Brighton school board voted unanimously to remove all sex education books from the high school

library. A member of the board's steering committee threatened legal action if the board did not vote to remove the books. According to her, the Michigan sex education law prohibits the instruction and dispensation of birth control information through the public schools.[16] The school's attorney told the board: "Taken to its logical conclusion, (the law) makes even the *Detroit Free Press* illegal in the library because it has small ads dealing with abortion clinics in it."[17] One board member condemned the expurgation of the sex education books by the member of the steering committee who allegedly mutilated the books before returning them to the school library.[18]

WYOMING, MICHIGAN. The principal of Wyoming High School ordered three copies of *Saturday Night Fever* removed from the school library, but he denied that he planned to have them burned. The head of the local Interfaith Committee Against Blasphemy complained about the book after his daughter brought it home. He wrote: "The four-letter words, along with some of the scenes described are bad enough, but to have the name of Almighty God blasphemed like it is, is repulsive." The book was one of several hundred paperbacks chosen for the library by students.[19]

PERU, ILLINOIS. The school board voted to ban *Scholastic Scope* magazine from the Peru schools. One board member complained that the magazine is "too negative and realistic" for sixth and seventh graders. She singled out an issue that contained Shirley Jackson's "The Lottery," and said that the story is "unnecessarily violent" and fails to present the "wrongness" of the people's stoning a woman to death. A board member who opposed the decision to discontinue the magazine pointed out that the Bible contains similar stories of stonings.[20]

KINGSPORT, TENNESSEE. The school board of Sullivan County took a five-minute recess to examine *Have Jumpshot, Will Travel* before deciding to remove it from all school libraries. The board acted upon the complaint of a parent who said the book was "purely pornographic," and he feared that as many as a thousand other "filthy" books were still in the school libraries.[21]

PINELLAS COUNTY, FLORIDA. The chairman of the Citizens Commission on Education asked the school board of Pinellas County to explain why Eric Partridge's *Dictionary of Slang and Unconventional English* was in the high school libraries. The chairman linked the presence of the book to 696 suspensions of students who used profanity. The chairman's complaint precipitated support of the dictionary by a number of individuals and professional organizations that noted the removal of the book "would constitute an infringement of the students' right to read."[22]

COBB COUNTY, GEORGIA. The school board of Cobb County removed several copies of Richard Dorson's *America in Legend* from school libraries because it "condones draft dodging," is "terrible for children," and contains several stanzas of "Casey Jones" that describes his sexual prowess. Board members were disturbed that the book had been purchased as a result of favorable reviews in professional publications. One board member suggested that, in the future, books should be read in their entirety before purchase because "you're going to get freaks in the American Library Association just like any place else."[23]

SAVANNAH, GEORGIA. The school board removed all copies of *A Hero Ain't Nothin' but a Sandwich* from all school libraries in Savannah. The president of the board called the book "garbage" and commented: "We don't need people going around and calling other people 'jive-asses' and saying, 'Fuck the society.' "[24]

COLUMBIA, SOUTH CAROLINA. The South Carolina Board of Education refused to approve two books recommended for remedial reading classes because they contained such words as *damn, hell,* and *by God.* One South Carolina official said that board approval of reading materials should "legitimize the language to be used by young people. The argument that people are using this language—including noted authors—doesn't justify the state's sanctioning it as language used by society."[25]

WILMINGTON, NORTH CAROLINA. The school board of New Hanover County voted four to two to retain *The Curious Eye,* an anthol-

ogy of short stories. Teachers and students staunchly defended the book, which was used as optional reading for junior and senior high school classes. Speaking about one of the stories that had been labeled obscene, a student said: "I find the poverty and despair described in the story obscene, not the words used to convey it."[26]

FAIRFAX COUNTY, VIRGINIA. After students in a high school government class had discussed the Nazi Party in Germany, had viewed films about the Nazis, and had discussed the television showing of *The Holocaust,* one student suggested that the class invite a member of the National Socialist White People's party to speak. An area superintendent first approved the request and then denied it because the local PTA recommended that the speaker not appear. "We felt there would be a lot of reverberations at the school as well as in the community," an officer of the PTA said.[27]

HERNDON, VIRGINIA. A parent's objection to the textbook *Hero/Anti-Hero,* was given to the book review committee for response. The committee voted unanimously to keep the anthology in the English curriculum of Herndon High School.[28] The complaining parent said that she would appeal the decision of the committee and that she protested the book for three reasons: (1) it takes the name of the Lord in vain; (2) it violates the Fairfax County Schools' Handbook for Secondary School Students Rights and Responsibilities which indicates that no student shall curse or use vulgar language nor be subjected to such language from any source; (3) it violates the laws of Herndon, where people are arrested and fined for saying words like *hell* and *damn* to a policeman or to their neighbors or families.[29]

HOWARD COUNTY, MARYLAND. Copies of a book describing the life of an aboriginal boy in Australia were removed from all elementary school libraries in Howard County. The reason given for the ban of Mary and Elizabeth Durack's *Kookanoo and the Kangaroo* is that it would be hard "for primary youngsters reading the book to make the distinction between the aborigines in Australia and black children in the U.S."[30]

The eleven-member review committee voted unanimously to remove the book because the illustrations depicted "black stereotyped features" and the word *piccaninny,* which means the child of one of the native people in Australia, has a pejorative meaning for Americans. The person who requested that the book be reviewed said that it would result in "a lessening of racial esteem for the black child."[31]

MIDDLETOWN, MARYLAND. Teachers can continue using Marjorie Kellogg's *Tell Me That You Love Me, Junie Moon* and John Gardner's *Grendel* in the English classes in Middletown High School. But *Grendel* was restricted for use by juniors and seniors who read *Beowulf.* The superintendent of Frederick County said that he, too, didn't like some of the language in the books but that the words were "used sparingly, without sensationalism, and within the context of the authors' purposes."[32]

A group calling itself Concerned Parents of Middleton Valley requested the banning of all books "containing obscene language or crude vulgarity." A leader of the group said that it was concerned with improving the curriculum not with censoring books.[33]

ROCKVILLE, MARYLAND. Working with librarians, the director of instructional materials removed *Sport* magazine from elementary and junior high school libraries in Montgomery County because of an issue devoted to sex in sports and because the "whole scope" of the magazine is adult.[34]

Members of Citizens United for Responsible Education (CURE) demanded that Gordon Parks' *The Learning Tree* be removed from high school libraries because of its "denigrating racial epithets toward both blacks and whites." The group also deplored the book's vulgar language and "cheap, explicit passages on sex."[35] In a statement in which he explained that the book would be kept in school libraries, the superintendent called it "a very moral book."[36]

Members of such organizations as CURE, Parents Who Care, and the National Organization for Women, which are very active in the Washington, D.C. area, had previously protested

the following materials used in the Montgomery County Schools: (1) the 1943 novel *Back to School with Betsy* because it contains "racial slurs"; (2) *The Sailor Dog,* which contains "atrocious grammatical sentence structure" (Born at sea in the teeth of a gale, the sailor was a dog. Scuppers was his name.); (3) *McBroom's Zoo* because it portrays hunters as "illiterate criminals who do not respect private property nor any wildlife"; (4) *Male and Female Under 18,* a collection of poetry that contains a poem written by a 15-year-old girl that "sets an extremely poor example as to what is acceptable" (See chap. 10); (5) *Russian Life Today,* a film criticized for its "omission of treatment of religious observances, especially Jews."[37]

EMPORIUM, PENNSYLVANIA. Author Daniel Keyes said that he was saddened by the removal of *Flowers for Algernon* from the eleventh grade classrooms in the Cameron County School District. A group of parents had protested to the school board that the book which inspired the making of the Academy Award-winning movie *Charly* was "sexually oriented."

"What bothers me is there's so little in the book to object to. The point of the book is love and compassion for one's fellow man," he said, adding that it had taken him eight years to write the novel about a mentally retarded man who overcame his problem with medicine, struggled to cope with an adult world, and then relapsed into retardation.[38]

OIL CITY, PENNSYLVANIA. During summer vacation the school board voted to remove John Steinbeck's *Of Mice and Men* from the school library and also drop it from the English curriculum. The board responded to parental complaints that the book "uses the Lord's name in vain, refers to prostitution, and takes a retarded person and makes a big issue of it." According to a school employee, most of the copies of the book, which had been in the school curriculum for five or six years, were burned.[39]

PHILADELPHIA, PENNSYLVANIA. Groups of German-Americans criticized the world history curriculum in the Philadelphia schools because it emphasized the extermination of European

Jews as a singular example of genocide. The spokesperson for thirty clubs with more than five thousand members said that the genocide during Hitler's reign "is too frequently stressed, while other examples of mass extermination are ignored." He feared that students would believe that genocide is only a Teutonic crime. An assistant superintendent replied that emphasis "placed on the Holocaust was justified because it was so recent and so sweeping."[40]

RED CROSS, PENNSYLVANIA. The board of directors of the Line Mountain School District ordered three books removed from the middle school library and destroyed. Responding to parental complaints about the books, the board committed these books to destruction: *Go Ask Alice, The Cheese Stands Alone,* and *Bonnie Jo, Go Home.*

Speaking about *Go Ask Alice,* the board president said: "It's a true story and it's very shocking. It contains language which is not fit for anyone, let alone children. Not only should it be banned, but it should be destroyed, because it's not fit to be around."[41] He had similar comments about *The Cheese Stands Alone.* Although he complimented *Bonnie Jo, Go Home,* he said the book must be banned for "just one error"—the condoning of abortion. "Abortion is murder. And I not only oppose murder but so does God and God's word says the destruction of life is murder."[42]

SELINSGROVE, PENNSYLVANIA. J. D. Salinger's *The Catcher in the Rye* can once again be on the suggested reading list for an English elective course entitled "Searching for Values and Identity Through Literature." In an earlier decision, the board of directors of the Selinsgrove Area School District voted five to four to remove the book from the course. But when it was discovered that the vote was invalid because school policy calls for a two-thirds vote for removal only after the superintendent calls for action, the board voted seven to two in favor of the book.[43]

SUNBURY, PENNSYLVANIA. The board of education of the Shikellamy School District approved Donald Hiatt's *True, False or In*

Between for the logic course in the high school. The book had been criticized for having a liberal bias.[44] A member of the lay advisory committee said the text had a distinct "political, liberal, social and humanistic bias." She said that the author urges readers not to use labels but then uses them himself. She stated that the author uses the late Senator Joseph McCarthy and the John Birch Society as "whipping boys." And, finally, she declared that the author claims that Christianity and communism cannot coexist in the world and that one philosophy will triumph.[45]

ELMWOOD PARK, NEW JERSEY. The school board of Elmwood Park rejected demands of a parent that Richard Wright's *Native Son* be removed from the reading list of a high school English honors class. The protesting parent wanted to read a three page list of profanity and "explicit sexuality" to the board, but the superintendent denied her request, noting that any parent could obtain a copy of the entire book and read it.

"There is no question but what the book is uncompromising in its narration. It is graphic, strong, and sometimes shocking in its presentation." But, the superintendent added, the book is considered to be a classic of American fiction.[46] The complaining parent said that the book does not fit the dictionary definition of a classic. "I feel that a book which uses God's name in vain . . . and describes prostitution is not indicative of the highest standard of lasting merit."[47]

MAHWAH, NEW JERSEY. The school board's decision to ban *American Civics* from the classroom precipitated so much protest that the board decided to restore the book. The *Bergen Record* commented that there is more to the world than Mahwah, New Jersey, and that the charge that the book gave a distorted view of America resulted from the school trustees' looking at the problems of the rest of the country as if they did not concern Mahwah.[48]

TRENTON, NEW JERSEY. A New Jersey Superior Court Judge decided that the principal of Princeton High School did not restrict the free speech of high school students when he ordered them to

delete certain words from the text of a play before performing it publicly. The judge said that he did not see how the educational benefit of *The Moon Children* would be "diluted by the fact that students were prevented from swearing on stage."[49]

WOODBURY, NEW JERSEY. The principal of Woodbury High School canceled a student production of David Rabe's *The Orphan,* a modern-day retelling of the Greek tragedy of King Agamemnon. Angry students declared that there is nothing obscene about the play and appealed the principal's decision to the school board. After reading the play, board members backed the principal and voted against the student production.[50]

BROCKPORT, NEW YORK. Students who have written permission may borrow Norma Klein's *Naomi in the Middle* from an elementary school library in Brockport. That method of borrowing the book represented the school board's compromise between banning it and keeping it on the open shelf. Even though he found parts of the book offensive and poorly written, the school superintendent said that school officials should not ban it. "I think that establishes a fairly dangerous precedent."[51]

LEVITTOWN, NEW YORK. Using a list of "objectionable books" prepared by an organization called Parents of New York—United (PONY-U), the school board of the Island Trees Union Free School District voted to remove these eleven books from school libraries: Anonymous, *Go Ask Alice;* Jerome W. Archer, editor, *A Reader for Writers;* Alice Childress, *A Hero Ain't Nothin' but a Sandwich;* Eldridge Cleaver, *Soul on Ice;* Langston Hughes. *Best Short Stories by Negro Writers;* Oliver La Farge, *Laughing Boy;* Bernard Malamud, *The Fixer;* Desmond Morris, *The Naked Ape;* Piri Thomas, *Down These Mean Streets;* Kurt Vonnegut, *Slaughterhouse Five;* Richard Wright, *Black Boy.*

According to the United Teachers of Island Trees, three school board members attended a conference in which they "learned of books found in schools throughout the country which were anti-American, anti-Christian, anti-Semitic and just plain

60

filthy."[52] Two board members entered a school library at night and looked through the card catalogue to determine that nine of the books were available. The board gave lists of the objectionable books to the school librarians and ordered them to remove the titles from the shelves. Upon learning that Bernard Malamud's *The Fixer* was used in an English class, the principal removed all copies from the classroom and storage closet. The two books available in the junior high school library, *Laughing Boy* and *A Reader for Writers,* were removed from the shelves.[53]

The school board did not follow its own policies for reviewing and removing books from classroom or library use. The board's action stirred enough people in the community that the board appointed a committee consisting of four parents and four teachers to review the books. As a result of the recommendations of the review committee, the board returned two titles— *Laughing Boy* and *Black Boy* to the school libraries—and removed all others, even though the committee voted in favor of *Go Ask Alice, The Fixer,* and *Best Short Stories by Negro Writers.* The board also restricted access to *Black Boy* to those students who had written permission from their parents to borrow the book.[54]

Five students in the Island Trees district filed suit against the school board in the United States District Court for the Eastern District of New York. The suit claims that the board, by removing nine books from school libraries, violated both New York and U.S. constitutional guarantees of freedom of expression.[55] In an *amicus* brief filed by the American Jewish Committee and other organizations, the authors of the brief note that they were astounded that *The Fixer* "was banned because it contained anti-Semitic references. That assertion can lead to only one of two conclusions: that its author is either illiterate or dishonest. *The Fixer* clearly condemns anti-Semitism, as it does the authoritarian society which is the seed bed of anti-Semitism."[56]

The brief also notes that *A Reader for Writers* was banned only because it contained Jonathan Swift's classic satire, "A Modest Proposal." The brief states: "It is unthinkable that, for example, a high school Honors English class should be denied

the right to have this literary masterpiece included in its curriculum."[57] The court has yet to hand down an opinion in this case which some First Amendment scholars consider to be one of the most important in the nation.

CHESTER, VERMONT. The school board of the Windsor Southwest School District voted to remove Norma Fox Mazer's *Saturday, the Twelfth of October* from the seventh grade classroom of Green Mountain Union School. The book deals with girls experiencing their first menstrual periods. A complaining parent called the book "filthy."[58]

NASHUA, NEW HAMPSHIRE. Parents of a ninth-grade student at Spring Street High School filed a formal complaint with the school board against the use of Richard Wright's *Black Boy* in English classes. As a result of the complaint, a review committee recommended that the book be removed from grade nine and be used only in elective classes in grades eleven and twelve.[59]

Controversies over *Black Boy* and *Ms.* magazine, which was banned by the Nashua school board,[60] have spread throughout New Hampshire. Groups calling themselves Concerned Parents and Taxpayers for Better Education have protested such diverse works as *Our Bodies, Ourselves, Of Mice and Men, The Catcher in the Rye,* and *Color, Communism and Common Sense.*[61] According to the National Congress of Educational Excellence, an NCEE member in New Hampshire spent much of 1977 "meeting with parents in the state to discuss issues such as textbook content, values and moral education and competency testing." Speaking to an overflow crowd at one workshop, the woman was quoted as having said: "Teachers are being paid for doing a job for children but are doing a job on our children . . . It's imperative that parents go to the schools and check out textbooks."[62]

In an article published in both the *Nashua Telegram* and the *Manchester Union Leader,* the NCEE member made these observations: "Our educational system leaves much to be desired and understandably so. In 10 years of school, a student will have received less than one year of the vital and everlasting

basics. Educators and School Boards are hell-bent on pushing the three "R's" further and further into the background in order to serve a special interest group.

Educators have completely lost sight of what makes up a good education. They would have us think that bigger schools, more personnel, an abundance of nonsensical curriculum, outrageous pay checks, permissiveness, arrogance on the part of the educational establishment and their non-productive innovations create quality education.

Close analysis will prove that what they are producing can be summed up in two words . . . arrogant illiterates."[63]

DYER BROOK, MAINE. High school students in six Aroostock County communities may read John Updike's *Rabbit Run*—if they have parental permission. "The school board voted eight to six against banning the book and seven to six to allow students to read the book after obtaining a permission slip from home." The book was placed on a reserved shelf in the library.[64]

NEW LISBON, MAINE. A teacher with twelve years of teaching experience at Lisbon High School became involved in a long and bitter battle over textbooks that resulted in the removal of five books from her elective classes in English. Early in 1977, the school committee voted to prohibit the teacher from using these three books in two of her classes: Michael Jacot's *The Last Butterfly*, Don Robertson's *Praise the Human Season,* and Megan Terry's *Calm Down Mother,* a collection of plays by and about women.[65]

Eight months later, the school board voted to remove Alexander Solzhenitsyn's *A Day in the Life of Ivan Denisovich* and Sylvia Plath's *The Bell Jar* from the teacher's optional course on death and dying. The board members banned the books from the course—but not from the school library—on the basis of "*New York Times* language guidelines," which the chairman of the school committee admitted that he and the other members of the committee had "never seen or studied."[66] "Board members did not reply to questions asking how books could be judged on the basis of guidelines which had not been studied or even obtained

by those involved in the decision." However, the chairman of the school committee said, "We have a pretty good idea of what gets into print, though."[67]

SANFORD, MAINE. The Sanford school committee voted four to one to bar from the high school all signs advertising birth control counseling or services. The dissenting member said that the board members were acting like ostriches with their heads in the sand when they hope that "our kids aren't going to become sexually active . . . but the fact is that some . . . have already made that decision."[68] The board decision served as approval of the school superintendent's removal of a poster advertising free contraceptive services and pregnancy counseling.[69]

TOWNSEND, MASSACHUSETTS. The president of the Massachusetts Chapter of the National Congress for Educational Excellence spoke to an audience of three hundred about humanistic education. She defined it as "a generic term for an ethical system whose basis is, 'The solution of man's problems is in man alone. This denies the existence of a Supreme Being.' " She added that the purpose of humanistic education is to change the child's attitudes. She said that a child is taught "to be answerable to his own conscience only, to a set of values which he alone devised."[70]

She told the audience that humanistic philosophy is closely allied to bizarre methods of sex education and to values clarification. In the latter programs there are "no taboos, restrictions, or morals." She said that a child gets the message that it is all right to lie and steal as long as no one is hurt. To counter humanism and values clarification, she urged parents to become aware of all programs taught in the schools and to counter them by insisting that their children's right of privacy not be invaded and by pointing out that the schools are teaching values and morals that are contrary to those taught in the home.[71]

PROVIDENCE, RHODE ISLAND. Poet James E. Humphrey received two threatening telephone calls as well as a letter stating: "We warn you. Don't teach or die." In his efforts to teach poetry at South Boston High School, the poet had used his latest book of

poems entitled *The Relearning*. Several teachers and a group of parents complained that the book is vulgar. Although he stopped using the book, which he says is written in a clean way and is not vulgar, the complaints continued and the threats were made.[72] *The Relearning* had been nominated for both the 1977 Pulitzer Prize and the National Book Award.

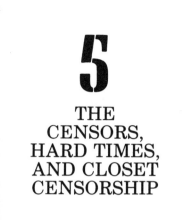

5
THE CENSORS, HARD TIMES, AND CLOSET CENSORSHIP

Those who bring textbook content to the public's attention are often referred to as "textbook censors." However, this is not true. Traditional American values are now being censored from textbooks even before they reach the reviewer.—Mel Gabler, co-founder of Educational Research Analysts[1]

I am a censor, and I'm proud of it. It's supposed to be a dirty word. I would rather say I'm trying to improve the quality of education. But if you want to call it censorship, fine. If you want to call it concern, fine.—Jil Wilson, founder of PARENTS (People of America Responding to Educational Needs of Today's Society)[2]

Edward Jenkinson refers to our objection to the use of pornography as "Go Ask Alice" in the classroom as censorship. This book was censored by the author who wrote it and the publisher who published it—they

66

filled it with gutter language stronger than hell and damn.—Sharon Lowry, secretary of People Who Care (Warsaw, Indiana)[3]

With the possible exception of the founder of PARENTS, most people who attempt to have books banned dislike being called censors. They maintain that as parents and/or concerned citizens they cannot be censors since they lack the authority to remove books from classrooms or library shelves. To support their contention, they frequently cite this dictionary definition of *censor*: "an official who examines books, plays, etc., for the purpose of suppressing parts deemed objectionable on moral, political, military, or other grounds." The book protesters seldom cite these two definitions of *censor*: "any person who supervises the manners or morality of others; an adverse critic—faultfinder."

Individuals and groups know that they do not have to be in positions of authority to have books banned from the public schools; rather, they know that in some school systems they simply need to exert sufficient pressure on school boards, school administrators, and/or clasroom teachers to realize their goal. They also know that they are more likely to be successful if they can rally a number of taxpayers to their cause by proclaiming that the textbooks or library books are anti-God, anti-American, anti-parent, and/or immoral. Finally, they know that even if they are not successful after their first or second attack on a book or books, they are very likely to win if they keep attacking on many fronts and tie the "objectionable" books or ideas to local or national problems that anger people.

The censors thrive on hard times. Few people would pay attention to them if there were no social, economic, moral, or political problems. Few people would pay attention if the schools were not under fire because of declining Scholastic Aptitude Test scores, rising illiteracy rates, escalating costs of education, and increasing concern about violence and vandalism in the schools. Few people would pay attention if contemporary authors did not use the language of the streets, of smoke-filled back rooms, and of real life to let their characters talk about the

world as they see it. Few people would pay attention if students had not protested in the sixties and if many people had not blamed the schools for the protests. And, finally, few people would pay attention if the schools did not experiment with curricula and with innovative programs to make education more meaningful for students.)

Hard times—real and imagined—have contributed to the sharp increase in censorship activity. But difficult conditions are not the only factors that precipitate attempts to rid the schools of "questionable" books, films, teaching methods, and other teaching materials. The following are some of the reasons that more people than ever before are attempting to "clean up" the schools:

1. The removal of prayer and Bible reading from the schools has disturbed thousands of people who are calling for a return to the "moral education" of the pre-World War II era. On the other hand, any mention of God or religion in the schools is anathema to the atheistic groups that monitor the schools.

2. The charge that the schools preach the religion of secular humanism has attracted considerable attention and has become one of the rallying cries of organizations that attempt to ban books, materials, and teaching methods that they brand as being secular humanistic. (See chap. 7 and 9.)

3. Innovative programs such as values clarification, drug education, and sex education anger some parents— especially those who believe that the schools are preaching secular humanism.

4. The combination of the first three reasons has led individuals and groups to attempt to remove everything they label secular humanistic from the schools. If they fail, they believe their only alternative is to establish private schools. For example, on at least two occasions, a minister with a national television congregation has urged his followers to "bring immoral public education to its knees by establishing between two and three thousand American Christian schools each year." More than seven hundred Christian schools were opened in 1977.

5. Several national and local organizations are using the back-to-basics movement as a convenient cover for their attempts to remove from the public schools much of contemporary literature as well as courses they don't like.

6. Contemporary writers—even authors of books for teenagers—treat subjects that were once considered taboo in language that some parents consider too realistic; consequently, several groups of concerned citizens have focused their attention on novels for adolescents.

7. Organizations like the Council on Interracial Books for Children and the National Organization for Women have expressed concern about books that contain racist or sexist statements. Such organizations have suggested guidelines for authors.

8. Anti-feminist organizations do not want women to be pictured as anything but housewives. In 1978 a group of textbook critics challenged a book that showed women in careers outside the home. "The idea expressed (by the textbook protesters) is that most women in this country are in the home—where they should be—and if they're to be portrayed accurately, that is what has to be shown."[4]

9. The emergence of black literature—some of which is written in black dialect—angers some parents. In Kanawha County, for example, spokespersons "for the anti-book movement vigorously denied that there was any element of racism in their protest or in their community—except, they alleged, in the 'racial hatred' portrayed in the books. If the protest movement and the community itself are as free from racial prejudice as its leaders claim, then Kanawha County, West Virginia, is indeed unique among all counties in this country. And if the protest is as free from racism as its leaders claim, then it is difficult to understand why teachers have received complaints from parents about illustrations in textbooks depicting a white female student and black male student together. Or why a minister was called by an irate parent who wanted to know if the minister wanted his daughter to marry a black man . . . Or why . . . a building in an outlying area of the county was painted with lettering that stated, 'Get the nigger books out!' "[5]

10. Adults who have had unpleasant experiences in school sometimes strike out because of past frustrations. In Kanawha County, for example, a former school official gave as one reason for the controversy "some protesters' own bad school experiences. At school the mountaineers were sometimes ridiculed, forced to drop out, and denied other avenues to gain needed skills."[6]

11. Parents sometimes become frustrated when they do not recognize the subject matter their children are studying. When they cannot help with homework because they do not understand the new math or a new approach to grammar, they might begin questioning the validity of what their children are studying. And when their children bring home literature that treats topics the parents will not discuss in a home, the adults sometimes become enraged and strike out against the books.

12. Parents frequently complain about the failure of educators to communicate effectively. Parents have not always been told the objectives of new programs or the reasons that specific books are used, and when they ask, they are sometimes put down by the school people. An officer of Parents of Minnesota, Inc. was quoted as having said: "We are constantly reminded that we don't have a degree. We'll be at a stalemate until we reach a point where educators stop being condescending and listen to parents' concerns. Education is kind of a sacred cow, and teachers are on a pedestal. If you disagree, there must be something wrong with you. You're crazy; a nut."[7]

13. Local and national organizations of concerned citizens have called attention to many school problems—real and imagined. The vocal organizations have given courage to many people who would have previously remained silent but who now protest books and materials. The organizations have also provided parents with reviews of books so that the parents can attempt to ban a specific work without having to read it. (See chaps. 8 and 9.)

14. Schools are a convenient target for unhappy citizens. Many people feel that they cannot fight Washington,

70

the state capitol, or even city hall. When they become un-happy because of inflation, federal or state laws, the so-called moral decline, or anything else, they want to lash out. But they don't always know how to attack the problems that really trouble them. So they vent their spleen upon the schools.

Whether elected or appointed, school boards must con-duct public meetings. Citizens who feel that they cannot fight Washington can complain to school boards because they are accessible. And the schools themselves are open every weekday, at least nine months out of the year. Parents can go to a school and demand to see the principal, and he or she cannot always refuse to see them. Nor can a classroom teacher refuse to see parents.

15. Because the media have given the schools so much publicity since the student protest movement of the sixties, taxpayers have a tendency to feel that almost everything that's wrong with society stems from the schools. The schools have become scapegoats and convenient targets for irate taxpayers, and censorship is one of their weapons.

Those are fifteen common reasons why more and more people are attempting to have books banned from classrooms and school libraries. But each censor has his or her own reasons for attacking books, films, magazines, homework assignments, or entire school programs. A characteristic of the censors is that they are absolutely certain that they are in the right, as Ken Donelson, Professor of English at Arizona State University and a prolific writer about censorship activity, points out: "The censor, however good and decent and sincere and religious and dedicated and patriotic, is usually supremely confident of his or her own rightness. The censor seems certain while the teacher can never be. The censor knows truth while the teacher is only trying to perceive it. The censor sometimes claims to have a direct pipeline to God and truth and right while the teacher can make no such sacrilegious assertion. The censor may claim that he knows what is good for every person while the teacher knows only that each of us must take a personal trip through this world

searching for the good. The censor can afford the luxury of arrogance and omniscience while the teacher can not so pretend."[8]

Censors frequently argue that what they are trying to do is no different from book selection. They argue that the line between censorship and selection is so fine that no one can distinguish between the two. In an article for the *Wilson Library Bulletin*, Lester Asheim made this distinction:

> Selection . . . begins with a presumption in favor of liberty of thought; censorship, with a presumption in favor of thought control. Selection's approach to the book is positive, seeking its value in the book as a book and in the book as a whole. Censorship's approach is negative, seeking for vulnerable characteristics wherever they can be found—anywhere within the book, or even outside it. Selection seeks to protect the right of the reader to read; censorship seeks to protect—not the right—but the reader himself from the fancied effects of his reading. The selector has faith in the intelligence of the reader; the censor has faith only in his own.
>
> In other words, selection is democratic while censorship is authoritarian, and in our democracy we have traditionally tended to put our trust in the selector rather than in the censor.[9]

An unpublished incident of censorship illustrates the distinction between selection and censorship. In a school system in Indiana, the elementary school teachers carefully examined the seven series of reading textbooks that had been placed on the State Textbook Adoption List. Knowing that they would have to use the selected series for five years until the State issued a new approved listed in reading, the teachers pored over the seven series, using a number of criteria in the selection process. When they finished their study, they all agreed on the same series and recommended to the superintendent that he purchase the books.

Hearing of the decision, a taxpayer in the community told the superintendent that she and her church would sue the school system if it purchased copies of the selected series. She noted two pictures in the books she considered offensive. One showed a young boy playing cards with an old man, perhaps his grandfather; the other showed a house made of cards. The woman said that cardplaying is evil and that the books should not be purchased because they were sinful. She repeated her threat to sue the school system. The superintendent then called in the teachers and told them they would have to use their second choice of reading series since he would not purchase the first one.

That is only one of hundreds of unpublished incidents of censorship that occur in the United States each year. Many go unreported because the teachers or librarians, as was the case in the incident reported above, are afraid to go to the parents in the community and to the media with their story. Many other incidents go unreported because no one outside the classroom or library knows about them. They are examples of closet censorship.

When a teacher reads that *The Catcher in the Rye,* for example, is being protested in a nearby community, he or she may decide not to teach that book again in fear of censorship. That is closet censorship. When a librarian fails to order a book because it has provoked criticism from irate taxpayers in other communities, that is closet censorship. When a department chairperson locks up all copies of John Steinbeck's *Of Mice and Men* because one parent quietly objected to the book, that's closet censorship. And when a teacher takes a felt-tip pen and marks out a word in all copies of an anthology, that's closet censorship.

Censors rarely consider the consequences of their actions. For example, the teacher who used a felt-tip pen to black the word *crap* out of anthologies would probably have been horrified to hear the words that students substituted for the missing one. The substitutions would unquestionably have been considered far more offensive by the teacher.

In nearly every community in which books have been

73

banned, the forbidden works become best sellers among students. As one teacher remarked, the best way to get students to read a book is to tell them they can't read it. Thus, when concerned citizens ban *Go Ask Alice, The Catcher in the Rye,* or a textbook, they turn the banned books into popular reading among teenagers. Perhaps if the censors were to rate all of Shakespeare's works "X," his plays would once again be widely read in the schools.

6

TARGETS
OF
THE
CENSORS

It is tempting to write only the word *everything* and call it chapter 6. If it would not be dismissed by readers as facetious, that one word chapter would summarize the targets of the censors. For no textbook, regardless how bland and inoffensive, escapes all potential censors. At least one parent objected to every one of the 325 textbooks that were recommended for adoption in Kanawha County. When textbooks are submitted for adoption in Texas, few do not become subjects of bills of particulars submitted by citizens who think the books should not be adopted.

But the targets of today's censors go far beyond textbooks. They include magazines, library books, dictionaries, teaching methods, homework assignments, films, pictures, and entire programs. Nothing is safe.

Dictionary definitions of the word *bed* frequently include "a place for lovemaking," "a marital relationship, with its rights and intimacies," and "to have sexual intercourse with."[1] Perhaps most people in the United States would not find those definitions unusual or unnerving, but a sufficient number of

citizens in at least four states have found those definitions, as well as other words and their definitions, offensive enough to warrant drastic action.

In June of 1976, the school board voted four to three to remove *The American Heritage Dictionary* from classrooms in Anchorage, Alaska. The decision was precipitated by complaints from a group of parents who called themselves People for Better Education. The organization found definitions for these words, among others, to be offensive: ass, tail, ball, bed, knocker, and nut.

When the parents complained about the *AHD,* the assistant superintendent appointed a review committee that examined the dictionary and approved it unanimously. Appearing before the school board, the assistant superintendent reported the findings of the committee, noted that "the ability of a child to look up 'dirty words' helped diffuse excitement and curiosity about them," and explained that the dictionary is "an excellent reference for advanced students, especially for scientific terms."

As the assistant superintendent presented his arguments, four members of the school board sat with a list of definitions in front of them. The four voted against the dictionary.[2]

Three months later, the school board voted to remove the *AHD* from the high school in Cedar Lake, Indiana. Parents complained that "seventy or eighty" words were obscene or otherwise inappropriate for high school students. *Bed* was one of the more frequently criticized entries. "We're not a bunch of weirdo book burners out here," explained one board member. "But we think this one [the *AHD*] goes too far."[3]

In mid-November, the Cedar Lake school board voted three to two to allow the dictionary to be used in senior English classrooms. Thus the school board reversed the position it had taken at an earlier meeting in November when it refused to lift the ban on the *AHD.* In the first meeting in November, the school board refused to apologize to teachers whom the president of the board "reportedly characterized as unqualified to select learning materials." The legal counsel advised the Cedar Lake school board that the *AHD* could not be considered obscene. Although he thought that the school board "could win a

76

test case to establish its authority to remove controversial material, such litigation would be too costly."[4]

In April of 1977, the school board voted to remove the *AHD* from a junior high school in Eldon, Missouri. Twenty-four parents filed a complaint noting that thirty-nine words in the dictionary are "objectionable." One parent in Eldon was reported as having said: "If people learn words like that it ought to be where you and I learned it—in the street and in the gutter."[5]

On November 12, 1976, the Commissioner of Education for the State of Texas removed these five dictionaries from the list recommended by the State Textbook Committee: *The American Heritage Dictionary of the English Language,* High School Edition; *The Doubleday Dictionary; The Random House College Dictionary,* Revised Edition; *Webster's New World Dictionary of the American Language,* College Edition; and *Webster's Seventh New Collegiate Dictionary.*

In his report to the State Board of Education, the commissioner explained that he had removed the five dictionaries from the recommended list because of these two sub-sections of the Texas State Textbook Adoption Proclamation:

1.7 Textbooks offered for adoption shall not include blatantly offensive language or illustrations.

1.8 Textbooks offered for adoption shall not present material which would cause embarrasing situations or interference in the learning atmosphere of the classroom.[6]

Four months before he announced that the five dictionaries would not be on the purchase list, the Texas Commissioner received bills of particulars from various groups of citizens about the dictionaries that had been submitted for adoption. Six of the cover letters for the bills of particulars that I examined cited the two sub-sections of the Texas proclamation as reasons why the dictionaries should not be adopted.

The chairperson of a textbook committee of a prominent organization of women wrote this about *Webster's New World Dictionary of the American Language:* "Reviewer is shocked

that a supposedly reputable publisher would offer for adoption a book which is debasing the English language. Students need the basics rather than sub-standard language.["]7

The chairperson of the organization's reviewing committee cited twenty-six words as examples of "the objectionable material in this book." The words and the reasons for the objections follow:

Word	*Reason for Objection*
across-the-board	Betting on horse racing in Texas is illegal
Arab	Incomplete definition
ass -2	unnecessary
attempt	ties word into subj of murder
banana republic	insulting to Latins
bawdy house	unnecessary
bed	Why is sexual intercourse mentioned?
the big house	slang—unnecessary
block busting	inaccurate and unnecessary
brain	Def. denotes violence
bucket	slang: the buttocks.
butt	slang: the buttox [sic]
clap -2	refers to a brothel (claper) and gonorrhea: slang.
coke	slang for cocaine
crocked	slang for intoxicated
deflower	to cause loss of virginity: slang?
fag	slang for male homosexual
fairy	same obj. as above
gay	same obj. as above
G-string	slang: unnecessary
hooker	slang for prostitute
horny	slang for sexually excited
john	slang for toilet
keister, keaster	slang for buttocks or rump
kinky	sexually abnormal: slang
knock	slang—to make pregnant[8]

With the exception of the above listing, the fourteen bills of particulars that I examined which objected to "blatantly offensive" language listed words like these: cunnilingus, fart, fuck,

piss, screw, and shit. Those are the obvious words that a person who would spend time searching through five dictionaries looking for dirty words might find. But the reviewers also found these specific definitions of certain words, among others, that they labeled "blatantly offensive language":

> bastard—a person regarded with contempt, hatred, pity, resentment, etc. or, sometimes, with playful affection; a vulgar usage
>
> bed & board—law. obligation of marriage
>
> bed—conjugal cohabitation or the right to it; the married state; the marital relationship; to have sexual intercourse with; a place for lovemaking
>
> boob—a female breast
>
> cherry—the hymen; virginity
>
> dyke—a female homosexual: lesbian
>
> faggot—a male homosexual
>
> head—slang. one who uses or is addicted to a drug
>
> horny—slang. sexually excited
>
> hot—slang. sexually excited
>
> john—slang. a customer of a prostitute
>
> knock—slang. to make pregnant
>
> queer—homosexual; a contemptuous term
>
> rubber—slang. a condom
>
> shack—shack up with (slang); to share living quarters with (one's lover)
>
> slut—a dirty, untidy woman; slattern; a sexually immoral woman
>
> tail—slang. the buttocks
>
> tail-end—colloquial. the buttocks
>
> tit—a breast[9]

After citizens file bills of particulars, the Texas adoption procedure calls for the publishers—if they so desire—to file answers to the bills with the Texas Commissioner of Education. Most of the publishers take time to respond because the Texas adoption means a great deal of money in sales. In the case of the dictionaries, the publishers filed answers in which they noted the purpose of a dictionary. Some explained the lexicographers' decisions to include—or not to include—taboo words. All answered specific charges to words, as this answer illustrates:

Many [of the words objected to] are indelicate or impolite; some are widely regarded as vulgar and are so noted; none are considered obscenities. Moreover, because of their frequent and documented occurrences in speech, and in books and periodicals that students are likely to meet, they warrant inclusion.

We would offer the following specific examples. The first objection is to the word *ass,* in the sense of "buttocks." This usage, however indelicate or vulgar it may be regarded as being, is not taboo and is, in fact, heard today on radio and television in such phrases as "to get off one's ass and start doing something." . . .

The objection to the sense of *bed* as "the scene of sexual intercourse or procreation" or in the verb form "to have sexual intercourse with" is puzzling, in view of its established literary use over the centuries, including uses by Shakespeare, Dryden, Steele, and the translators of the King James Version of the Bible (see, for example, *Hebrews* 13:4). Similarly *fart* occurs frequently in literature, from Chaucer's *The Miller's Tale* onward, as do *bastard* and *hot.*

The citations in our file for such terms as *horny, faggot, frigging, shack up, knock up, hump,* and the other vulgar or indelicate usages on the list come from such publications as the *New York Times, Time Magazine, The New Yorker, Atlantic Monthly, Harper's, Saturday Review,* among many others, and in hundreds of books published by such highly reputable publishers as Atheneum, Coward-McCann, Little, Brown, Farrar, Straus & Giroux, McGraw-Hill, Stein & Day, Random House, Doubleday, and many others.[10]

That answer is representative of the answers filed with the Texas Commissioner of Education by the publishers of the five

80

dictionaries. But the answers were filed in vain; the dictionaries were placed on the no-purchase list.

Objections to the five dictionaries were not limited to protests about the so-called dirty words. The National Organization for Women (NOW) also filed bills of particulars. Those which I examined included an enumeration of the male and female staff members who worked on the dictionaries. The listing was usually followed by a note like this: "There are fewer women than men on the staff and they are concentrated in the lower positions." Then NOW's bills of particulars contained examples of objections to specific words or definitions. The following is a representative sampling:

"woman . . . 5. a man with qualities conventionally regarded as feminine, such as weakness, timidity, inclination to gossip, etc."

"womanish . . . suggests the faults that are regarded as characteristic of women."

Compare these unflattering definitions with "womanly", usually a positive term, which has no examples of qualities given.

"machismo . . . strong and assertive masculinity, characterized by virility, courage, aggressiveness, etc."

"macho . . . a strong, virile man—adj. masculine, virile, courageous, etc."

No negative connotations noted.

"Chairperson" not listed.

"Chairwoman" is only a run-on under "chairman."

The biographical entries leave something to be desired. Where are Mary McLeod Bethune, Margot Fonteyn, Emma Goldman, the Grimke sisters, Karen

Horney, Doris Lessing, Golda Meir, Louise Nevelson, Sylvia Plath, Leontyne Price and Beverly Sills, to cite just a few of the women who should be included and are not?"[11]

A dictionary is probably the most important book students will use to help them learn about the language they speak and write. It is a record of the words—good and bad—that people use. It is an indispensable tool for students. Unfortunately for those who would protect children from the world or who would right all wrongs by changing language, a dictionary records how people use words and what words they write and say. Thus, in any listing of approximately 150,000 words, there will be some that deal with the harsh realities of life. The protectors of the young will not keep teenagers from facing those realities or from hearing or reading the words by removing dictionaries from the schools.

An examination of hundreds of pages of materials distributed by organizations that attempt to censor textbooks and other materials, as well as an examination of hundreds of censorship incidents, yields these frequent targets of the censors:

1. Profanity. The censors seem to use this word to refer to more than language that takes the name of the Lord in vain. The word is used to refer to any word that the censors consider offensive.

2. Suggestive titles. One school board placed *Making It with Mademoiselle* on a list of books to be checked out by school librarians for possible removal. The book was removed from the list when the board members discovered it was a pattern book.[12]

A woman protested the book, *Belly Button Defense,* because of its title. It is a book for basketball coaches.

3. Drug education courses. Some pressure groups contend that incidents of drug use rise sharply after students take courses in drug education.

4. Sex education courses. One vocal critic of education calls sex education "how-to courses."[13]

5. Values clarification. The co-founder of a textbook

82

review clearing house wrote: "Even proponents of Values Clarification concede that it is based entirely upon relativism or 'situation ethics' (the philosophy that circumstances determine whether an action is right or wrong). Granted, some students may select absolute, moral positions; but since teachers are prohibited from favoring any moral stand, decisions will be heavily influenced by peer group knowledge and peer pressure. How many students will be able to stand firm in their religious faith while being constantly confronted by relativism in a public school classroom? . . . Thus, in practice, Values Clarification DESTROYS HOME TAUGHT VALUES."[14]

6. Assignments that are called invasions of privacy. The pressure groups dislike any classroom or homework assignments that call for students to express opinions that are based on their family background. The critics also abhor assignments that call for students to write or talk about their families.

7. Materials that defame historical personalities. Some of the critics do not want any negative traits of any of the nation's heroes mentioned in textbooks or discussed in class.

8. Ethnic studies. Some groups consider ethnic studies to be un-american.

9. Pagan cultures and life styles. One organization maintains that the study of pagan cultures is actually an attempt by teachers and textbook writers to promote such cultures and life styles.

10. Novels for adolescents. The organized censors do not approve of the subjects that novelists select today for treatment in stories for teenagers. Parents prone to censor books do not think their children should be reading Paul Zindel's *The Pigman,* S. E. Hinton's *The Outsiders,* John Donovan's *I'll Get There. It Better Be Worth The Trip;* Nat Hentoff's *I'm Really Dragged But Nothing Gets Me Down,* Paul Zindel's *My Darling, My Hamburger,* Judy Blume's *Are You There God? It's Me, Margaret,* and dozens of other popular books. Many protective parents do not want their sons and daughters reading books about student con-

flicts with parents, drug use and abuse, sex, homosexuality, teenage violence, the horrors of the ghetto, teenage pregnancy, and so forth. Such parents seem to remember the books they read when they were young, and they want the schools to focus attention on those books. Thus, the irate parents would have the schools remove the works of such authors as Judy Blume, Nat Hentoff, and Paul Zindel and replace them with the novels of Betty Cavanna, Anne Emery, Rosamund DuJardin, and John R. Tunis.

11. Realistic dialogue. Proponents of the back-to-basics movement do not want their children reading sentences that are not grammatically correct. Thus, they object to stories in which authors have characters speak substandard English. In other words, some censors believe that all characters in all books must speak standard English at all times. Otherwise, the censors contend, their children will be taught to use sub-standard English since they will imitate the language of the characters in books.

12. The works of questionable writers. The organized censors have a tendency to label authors as questionable if the censors do not agree with the ideas of the writers. The organized censors decry anthologies that contain stories, poems, and essays by such writers as Langston Hughes, Dick Gregory, Ogden Nash, Richard Wright, Joan Baez, and Malcolm X. Such writers are also labeled subversive, and the censors do not think that children should read any of their works.

13. The literature of homosexuals. Here is a portion of a message distributed by members of a Save Our Children group:

SAVE OUR CHILDREN wishes to thank those members of your community who, with their contributions, helped sweep us to victory in Florida. The battle has only begun, however, and soon we will carry our campaign all over the nation . . . For years homosexuals have been hogging the news with their

demands for equal rights, and it is time we pushed back. It is time that, along with thieves and murderers, they be branded for the sinners they are and removed from society ... You can fight to eliminate homosexual literature from our schools and libraries. This includes works by such homosexuals as:

Emily Dickinson	Andre Gide
Willa Cather	Jean Cocteau
Tennessee Williams	Gore Vidal
Oscar Wilde	John Milton
T. E. Lawrence	Hans Christian Andersen
Jean Genet	Marcel Proust
Gertrude Stein	Horatio Alger Jr.
Virginia Woolf	Truman Capote
Walt Whitman	Rod McKuen

14. Trash. Books that are frequently labeled trash include *The Catcher in the Rye, Flowers for Algernon, Soul on Ice, Forever, Black Boy, Laughing Boy, Go Ask Alice,* and most contemporary novels for adolescents.

15. Ideas, teaching methods, and books that are examples of secular humanism. (See chap. 7.)

16. The humanities, behavior modification, and human development. Concerned parents can obtain petitions that they can present to an administrator or teacher that call for the removal of their children from classes in which a variety of topics are discussed or a variety of methods are used. This petition, or a variation of it, was presented to teachers and/or administrators in Tulsa, Oklahoma in 1975, in Culver, Indiana in 1976, in Deer River, Minnesota in 1977, and in Austin, Texas in 1977:

This letter is to inform you that certain rights and privileges with regard to the instruction of our child———are permanently and specifically reserved by us, the parent(s). The familial relationship involving personal relationships, attitudes, responsibilities,

85

and religious and social training are the sole preroga-
tive of the parents.

Therefore, you are herby notified that our
child———will not be enrolled, instructed, or made to
participate in any course or class, workshop, study
group, etc. which includes: instruction in any training
or education in sex and/or sexual attitudes, personal
and family emotional development, introspective
examination of social and cultural aspects of family
life, group therapy or group criticism of family life,
"sensitivity training," "magic circles," Human Development programs, social awareness, self-awareness
or self-understanding, situation ethics, value judgment, values clarification, moral value alteration, Behavior Modification, Reality Therapy, ethnic studies,
"Humanities," the philosophies of the Humanist religion, the Occult, or any combination or degree thereof,
without the consent of the undersigned by express
written and signed permission.

17. Role playing. In Park Rapids, Minnesota, parents
attending a meeting of concerned citizens received a set of
guidelines for the selection of public school material that
included this statement: "Classroom materials, text books,
etc., must not use psycho-drama (role playing) as a teaching
tool."

18. Materials that contain negative statements about
parents. The guidelines distributed at a meeting in Park
Rapids, Minnesota noted that classroom "materials,
textbooks, audio and/or visual aids must not portray parents
as unloving, stupid, hypocritical, old fashioned, possessive
nor in any other negative way." Similar statements have
been made by censors elsewhere in the United States.

19. Phase-elective English programs. Proponents of
the back-to-basics movement are calling for the abolition of

phase-elective programs. People who cannot even describe phase-elective programs are blaming them for the declining SAT scores, for the failure of Johnny to write well, and for the failure of Susie to read well.

20. Sexist stereotypes. Members of the feminist movement are objecting to school materials that stereotype women.

21. Racist statements. The Council on Interracial Books for Children has objected to books that contain racial slurs. The council has actively campaigned for fairer treatment of all races in textbooks, and it encourages its book reviewers to "explore the 'hidden messages' " that every author transmits to young people.

22. Magazines that report the harsh realities of life. Censors have objected to *Time, Newsweek,* and *U.S. News and World Report* because they publish stories about war, crime, death, violence, and sex. Some censors do not want those magazines in school libraries.

23. Nudity. Textbook critics have expressed offense at reproductions of Michaelangelo's "The Creation," at a picture of a nude boy in Maurice Sendak's *In the Night Kitchen,* and at pictures of models in bathing suits in *Sports Illustrated.*

Those are only twenty-three targets of the censors. There are more. For example, Norma and Mel Gabler do not write all of the textbook reviews that they distribute through Educational Research Analysts. Instead, they invite concerned parents to write reviews for distribution by ERA. To provide a degree of uniformity in the reviews, the Gablers send concerned parents a three-page outline that lists these ten categories the reviewers should use for summarizing objectionable content in textbooks: (1.) Attacks on Values; (2.) Distorted Content; (3.) Negative Thinking; (4.) Violence; (5.) Academic Unexcellence; (6.) ISMS Fostered (Communism, Socialism, Internationalism); (7.) Invasions of Privacy; (8.) Behavioral Modification; (9.) Humanism, Occult, and other Religions Encouraged; (10.) Other important Educational Aspects.[15]

After several readings of the reviews that the Gablers

mailed to a concerned parent who was interested in the Ginn 360 Reading Series, among others, I followed the outline to find representative objections. The objections are recorded here exactly as they appear in the review. If an objectionable passage is cited by the review, that is noted here. The objections are recorded according to sub-headings in the outline.

ATTACK ON FAMILY, HOME, AND ADULTS. In Ginn 360, stories are presented which depict parents as stupid and idiotic, such as in "The Reluctant Dragon" (Level 12), when the son knows more than the parents; and, again, in the story "Curtains for Joy" (Level 12), where the antics of the children save the parents from looking stupid. To further have children doubting parents, stories where children solve adult problems are presented, such as "The New Fence" (Level 6) in which the objective is clearly stated: "Understanding that children can help adults solve problems."[16]

ATTACK ON AUTHORITY OF ESTABLISHED LAW AND ORDER. T.E. (teacher's edition of *To Turn a Stone*) p. 37, col. 1, Lines 4–5 & 8, Charley brought tobacco to George. OBJECTION: There are still many laws prohibiting minors from purchasing tobacco. This suggestion minimizes the law.[17] (Author's comment: In the story, "The Cave," Charley takes a "pocketful of tobacco from his dad's stock" to the old man who lives in a cave. Charley does not buy the tobacco. But the reviewer would not know that since he or she did not read the actual story before objecting to it. Rather, the reviewer notes at the beginning of the objections to *To Turn a Stone:* "It is difficult to form a rigid opinion of the book TO TURN A STONE with only the teacher's edition. Stories the students read are omitted and only summaries are written in their place.")

ATTACK ON BIBLE AND CHRISTIANITY. See p. 138 (of *Man the Myth-maker*), Question 1, "How is Deirdre like Pandora and Eve? . . ." OBJECTION: This last comparison between Pandora and Eve misleads the student into erroneous beliefs that Eve's story was mythical.[18]

ATTACK ON COUNTRY. Pp. 69–86 (of *Speculations*), Title: "Eastward Ho!" OBJECTION: This story is a parody on the history of the U.S. The Indians dominate the whites who eventually leave the crumpled remains of America for Europe where they hope to discover "a world of freedom." Depreciates U.S. history.[19]

ATTACK ON MORALITY—STEALING. T.E. (of *To Turn A Stone*) p. 300, col. 2, #6, "There are some people who would censor the tales of Robin Hood, for they do seem to support an outlaw and make the life of crime seem glamorous. It is shown in this story, however, that Robin Hood felt he did not have recourse to justice. . ." OBJECTION: Stealing and highway robbery is [sic] wrong any way you look at it. The end does not always justify the means.[20]

ATTACK ON FIXED VALUES CENSORED—QUESTIONS WITH NO FIRM ANSWER. P. 39 (of *Speculations*), Topic 2, "Plan a panel discussion based on the following topic: Computers are incapable of creative thinking and cannot replace man." OBJECTION: Infers [sic] that there can be more than 1 answer.[21]

DISTORTED CONTENT—ERRORS OF FACT. P. 224 (of *Man the Myth-maker*), SE (student edition) bottom, " 'No one I've ever known is what he appears to be on the surface.' Could Charlie's statement suggest that life consists of many kinds of metamorphoses?" OBJECTION: The text is

trying to stress change as being the major thing in life. This is not true. Change has no reliability; it cause [*sic*] the personality to be shattered. Remember that the word used in this assignment is "metamorphoses."[22]

NEGATIVE THINKING—ALIENATION. Story Title—Punk Takes a Stand. USING CREATIVE DRAMATICS. Teacher's Manual (for *On the Edge*—Page 251 Punk's problem should remind pupils of similar experiences when they had to "take a stand." Encourage the pupils to interpret these experiences through creative dramatics. OBJECTION: No wonder students are "taking a stand" today! They're being encouraged to in their textbooks![23]

NEGATIVE THINKING—DEPRESSING. P. 7, par. 1 (of teacher's manual for *Man in Literature*[24]), "We wish to present literature as something more than a portrait of the moralistic, the pretty, the sentimental, which often characterized the literature curriculum of earlier times. Much of the literature in the program is modern; a large bulk of it has been written since World War II. Although a great deal of older material is totally valid and relevant, we felt that the works of post-war writers speak more directly on the problems and circumstances of man today. Admittedly, much of this literature is harsh, gloomy, pessimistic; yet we cannot deny the accuracy of its reflections, the pertinency of its statements." OBJECTION: This statement prepares us for what is ahead. The text admits that the reading material will be depressing yet the authors choose to inflict it upon students. Most psychologists will readily agree that the high school years are hard enough to face for many young adults without having to be loaded down with the world's problems. Perhaps this is the reason

why suicide is still the number 1 killer among teen-agers today. It is a recent rediscovery that "children become what they learn."

Also, notice the authors state that the program concentrates on modern world literature. While it is obvious that all things new are not bad, neither is it obvious that they are all good. Conversely, everything old is not "out of touch" with modern problems just because it is old. For instance, the Bible is somewhere around 4,000 years old but it is still a very topical book to study for current problems. Therefore, the program is based on a philosophy that is not, in the most part, justified.

NEGATIVE THINKING—FRIGHTENING AND HORRIFYING. T.E. (of *To Turn a Stone*) p. 115, col. 1, "The Invisible Man" para 2, line [*sic*] 7–9. "Therefore he proposed that Dr. Kemp become his accomplice and that together they establish a reign of terror in order to eventually rule the world." OBJECTION: How cheerful and challenging! Don't you wish this were the motive behind all children's stories. Or, do you?[25]

NEGATIVE THINKING—PREJUDICIAL. Story Title—"The Trouble." Reviewer's parenthetical note: This story can be found in the 1970 copyright edition; however, has been left out of the 1973 copyright edition.

STUDENT TEXTBOOK—Page 72. "There was a riot on our block, and there were a lot of whites doing most of the shooting. Sometimes some blacks would come by with guns, but not often; they mostly had clubs." OBJECTION: Infers [*sic*] that whites are bad and blacks are good. Talk about discrimination! There is no story in this series that depicts the reverse![26]

91

NEGATIVE THINKING—SKEPTICAL. T.E. (of *To Turn a Stone*) p. 106, col. 1, para. 4, lines 1–2, "There's a sucker born every minute." OBJECTION: The P.T. Barnum philosophy is sceptical [*sic*]. This is a depressing thought.[27]

VIOLENCE. Firstly, the author, Mr. Peckinpah, is a noted violence writer, producer, and director. In Hollywood, he has produced and directed such ultra-violent and controversial films as "Straw Dogs" and "The Getaway." Death by violence seems to be a preoccupation with Peckinpah. When Sally Struthers, an actress, who appeared in "Straw Dogs" first met him, he was "throwing knives at a wall." Violence may be good for Peckinpah financially, but is it good in these new educational texts where violence is the norm and not the exception?[28]

VIOLENCE—CIVIL STRIFE. (Condone [*sic*] rebellion—anarchism, demonstrations, riots). P. TE9 (*Rebels*), par. 1, lines 1–4, "One of the most enduring methods for effecting change is rebellion. The U.S. has arrived at some of its most precious freedoms through acts of rebellion." OBJECTION: Most young people's concept of rebellion is activist, protest, defience [*sic*] of law, etc. This equates present day revolutionaries with our American Revolution. Should be deleted.[29]

ACADEMIC UNEXCELLENCE—Foolishness. Pp. 43–45 (of *Speculations*), "Buck Rogers." OBJECTION: 13 pages given to comic strip.[30]

ACADEMIC UNEXCELLENCE—Inappropriate content and pictures. Pp. 21–29 (of *Questions*), pictures. OBJECTION: Pictures with no identification. This is an 8th grade reader; not just pictures.[31]

ACADEMIC UNEXCELLENCE—Inappropriate content and pictures. P. 30 (of *Questions*) "Cuadrodos y Angulos." OBJECTION: What is the purpose of having the poem printed in Spanish?[32]
(Author's comment: This edition of the text was presented for adoption in Texas.)

ACADEMIC UNEXCELLENCE—Irrelevant content. P. 128, last par. (of *Pursuits*) "How would you explain the origin of the names of such singing groups as The Fifth Dimension, The Rolling Stones, The Jefferson Airplane, The Platters, Moby Grape, Quicksilver Messenger Service, or Big Brother and the Holding Company?" OBJECTION: This type of exercise has little or nothing to do with reading—it is pure speculation.[33]

ACADEMIC UNEXCELLENCE—Nonsense content. Pp. 95–128 (of *Pursuits*), Singers and Songs. OBJECTION: Too many pages (33 pages) given to songs and singers. Very little education value for students.[34]

ISMS FOSTERED—Communism not treated realistically (too favorable). T.E. (of *To Turn a Stone*) p. 187, ". . . Of An Organization" concentrates on the promotion of UNICEF. OBJECTION: UNICEF is a known Communist front. See "Fact Finder," Oct. 16, 1969. Vol. 27, Number 23 from Phoenix, Arizona.[35]

ISMS FOSTERED—Socialism, T.E. (of *To Turn a Stone*) p. 281, col. 1, #3, lines 5–9, "When the Law of Love works, each one considers his neighbors' needs in the same way as he considers his own. In such a situation there is no need to steal or kill since the good life is available for all. As long as people's needs are satisfied, there is little ruling that needs to be done." OBJECTION: If the above could be accomplished the situation would be ideal but it has not. The theory is

socialism and proves impossible. Children deserve to be informed of this.[36]

INVASIONS OF PRIVACY. Teacher's Manual—Page 195 (for *Helicopters and Gingerbread*). RELATED LANGUAGE ACTIVITIES. Use the following questions to encourage creative thinking and expression: If you could choose, would you rather be a parrot or a seal? Why? Would you rather live in a jungle or a zoo? Why? Would you like to live in someone's house? Why? Would you rather live on a mountain or near the ocean? Why? What would be the hardest thing for you to do? (accept imaginative ideas.) What would be the easiest thing for you to do? OBJECTION: Even as early as 1st grade, children expose their innermost feelings before the group.[37]

HUMANISM. TEACHER'S MANUAL—Page 147 (for *On the Edge*). Part II. 4. *Humanism* is an attitude about life that centers on human values. OBJECTION: Constantly throughout the stories, situation ethics which is the morality of the religion of Humanism is offered. Now we even find the definition of Humanism. Nowhere is the definition of Christianity given. What ever happened to "equality"?[38]

7

SECULAR
HUMANISM

The Random House Dictionary of the English Language— College Edition gives the following as the first three definitions of *secular:*

    1. of or pertaining to wordly things that are not re- garded as religious, spiritual, or sacred; temporal;
    2. not pertaining to or connected with religion (opposed to *sacred*); *secular music;*
    3. (of education, a school, etc.) concerned with non- religious subjects.

Webster's New World Dictionary of the American Language—College Edition gives the following definitions of *humanism:*

    1. the quality of being human; human nature;
    2. any system or way of thought or action concerned with the interests and ideals of people;
    3. the study of the humanities;

4. [H-], the intellectual and cultural movement that stemmed from the study of classical Greek and Latin literature and culture during the Middle Ages and was one of the factors giving rise to the Renaissance; it was characterized by an emphasis on human interests rather than on the natural world or religion.

The compounding of those two words has resulted in a battle cry that echos throughout the land wherever organizations determined to change the public schools are heard. To their way of thinking, secular humanism will destroy youth and, ultimately, the United States. The organizations fear "evil" Secular Humanism, as these quotations illustrate:

> The humanist educators have taken it upon themselves, without your consent, to change the attitudes of your children in regard to God, Family, and County [*sic*]. For example, most all social studies textbooks published today state in the preface and in the teacher's manual that it is necessary for the child to unlearn his old values; he comes to school "damaged by the concepts he has received during the first five years of life, and requires mental healing."—Representative John R. Rarick of Louisiana in a reprint distributed by The Network of Patriotic Letter Writers[1]

> Now the public school is making a frontal attack on Protestant ethics. And they [*sic*] make their attack by using our children; the young are grist for their mills, and the young come from us. They use our children to form a secular-humanist America.—from "A Christian Mother's View of the Values Clarification Program"[2]

> In light of the ban on prayer in public schools, it is incredible that the principles of Godless Secular Humanism have become the basis for much of public education. To committed Christians and those who

uphold our Judeo-Christian ethic, it is an intolerable tragedy and the ultimate hoax of modern times.—from *The Barbara M. Morris Report*[3]

(Parents, teachers, and citizens across the nation, concerned with the drift in the tax-supported schools toward humanistic education and academic decline, are confronting the question in their local communities, in the Courts, and in the halls of Congress. The public is growing more aware of the inequity of using tax dollars for the support of nontheistic religion. Secular humanism in the schools is indeed an issue whose time has come.—Onalee McGraw in a publication distributed by The Heritage Foundation[4]

Textbook content was gradually redirected to a collectivist philosophy. Christian/moral content has gradually been eliminated, till today textbooks are nearly 100% amoral or humanistic even though two U.S. Supreme Court rulings (1961 Torcaso case; 1964 Seegar [*sic*] case) stated that humanism is a religion. It is evident that our nation has directly followed this path toward amoralism and humanism. Thus it is vital that concerned citizens work to correct distorted textbook content.—the Mel Gablers, founders of Educational Research Analysts, in Appendix X of *Textbooks on Trial*[5])

We need to conclude with one singular inescapable fact: dialectical materialism, and Darwinism, have exceedingly strong roots in both Hedonism and Humanism, for both Hedonism and Humanism have flowered and taken on vigorous life under the later thesis and antithesis of dialectical materialism. Each is firmly and unmistakably interconnected, for the latter evolved from the former, and it is the whole of the philosophies of Hedonism, Humanism, Darwinism and dialectical materialism which run rife throughout large segments of that system of progressive education, which includes various social studies courses, as well as studies in the humanities.—Mary Royer in *Public Education: River of Pollution*[6]

The easiest way to seize control of a nation is to change the religion of the people. Once that is accomplished, the political aspects of the takeover fall readily into place.

That is the message of the battle taking place in public school systems all over the United States—since the tax supported schools have become the leading vanguard of the new religion.—John Steinbacher in an article reprinted by Young Parents Alert[7]

The organizations which believe that Secular Humanism is the religion of the public schools frequently cite two Supreme Court cases as evidence that it is a religion. The first case, *Torcaso* v. *Watkins*,[8] involved a man who had been appointed "to the office of Notary Public by the Governor of Maryland but was refused a commission to serve because he would not declare his belief in God." He filed suit to compel issuance of his commission, "charging that the State's requirements that he declare this belief violated 'the First and Fourteenth Amendments to the Constitution of the United States.'"[9]

In finding for Torcaso and declaring the Maryland religious test unconstitutional, the Supreme Court stated in its opinion:

We repeat and again reaffirm that neither a State nor the Federal Government can constitutionally force a person "to profess a belief or disbelief in any religion." Neither can constitutionally pass laws or impose requirements which aid all religions as against non-believers, and neither can aid those religions based on a belief in the existence of God as against those religions founded on different beliefs.[10]

That paragraph has obviously been deemed significant by the anti-Secular Humanists since it is the source of a footnote they cite as proof that the Supreme Court declared Secular Humanism to be a religion. The footnote in *Torcaso* v. *Watkins* refers to the last clause in the quoted paragraph above. The footnote follows in its entirety:

Among religions in this country which do not teach what would generally be considered a belief in the existence of God are Buddhism, Taoism, Ethical Culture, Secular Humanism and others. See *Washington Ethical Society* v. *District of Columbia,* 101 U.S. App. D.C. 371, 249 F. 2d 127; *Fellowship of Humanity* v. *County of Alameda,* 153 Cal. App. 2d 673, 315 P. 2d 394; II Encyclopaedia of the Social Sciences 293; 4 Encyclopaedia Britannica (1957 ed.) 325–327; 21 *id.,* at 797; Archer, Faiths Men Live By (2d ed. revised by Purinton), 120–138, 254–313; 1961 World Almanac 695, 712; Year Book of American Churches for 1961, at 29, 47.[11]

The second Supreme Court case that the anti-Secular Humanists cite is *United States* v. *Seeger.*[12] The Supreme Court agreed to hear the case of Seeger and two other conscientious objectors who did not want to serve in the armed forces but who did not specify that they believed in a Supreme Being; however, they indicated that they did believe in a religion. In upholding the decision of a lower court that Seeger was, indeed, a conscientious objector on religious grounds, the Supreme Court noted: "It may be that Seeger did not clearly demonstrate what his beliefs were with regard to the usual understanding of the term 'Supreme Being.' But as we have said Congress did not intend that to be the test."[13]

In the majority opinion, the Supreme Court made the following interesting observation:

Few would quarrel, we think, with the proposition that in no field of human endeavor has the tool of language proved so inadequate in the communication of ideas as it has in dealing with the fundamental questions of man's predicament in life, in death or in final judgment and retribution. This fact makes the task of discerning the intent of Congress in using the phrase "Supreme Being" a complex one. Nor is it made the easier by the richness and variety of spiritual life in our country/Over 250 sects inhabit our land. Some believe in a purely personal God, some in a super-natural deity; others think of religion as a way of life envisioning as its ultimate goal the day when all men can live together in perfect understanding and peace. There are those who think of God as the depth of our being; others, such as the Buddhists, strive for a state of lasting rest through self-denial and inner purifica-tion; in Hindu Philosophy, the Supreme Being is the transcendental reality which is truth, knowledge and bliss . . . This vast panoply of beliefs reveals the mag-nitude of the problem which faced the Congress when it set about providing an exemption from armed ser-vice. It also emphasizes the care that Congress realized was necessary in the fashioning of an exemp-tion which would be in keeping with its long-established policy of not picking and choosing among religious beliefs.[14]

But as interesting as the Seeger case is for that and other paragraphs on religion and for its decision on conscientious objection, it yields little information on Secular Humanism. In fact, there is absolutely no mention of Secular Humanism. But the opponents of the religion may have seized upon a footnote in the Seeger case to prove that the Court declared Secular Humanism to be a religion. That footnote follows in its entirely: "If he were an atheist, quite different problems would be pre-sented. Cf. *Torcaso* v. *Watkins,* 367 U.S. 488."[15]

That footnote refers to the first clause in the fourth sentence of this paragraph of the concurring opinion written by Justice William O. Douglas:

When the Congress spoke in the vague general terms of a Supreme Being I cannot, therefore, assume that it was so parochial as to use the words in the narrow sense urged on us. I would attribute tolerance and sophistication to the Congress, commensurate with the religious complexion of our communities. In sum, I agree with the Court that any person opposed to war on the basis of a sincere belief, which in his life fills the same place as a belief in God fills in the life of an orthodox religionist, is entitled to exemption under the statute. None comes to us an avowedly irreligious person or as an atheist; one, as a sincere believer in "goodness and virtue for their own sakes." His questions and doubts on theological issues and his wonder, and no more alien to the statutory standard than are the awe-inspired questions of a devout Buddhist.[16]

Thus, footnotes in two court decisions have given anti-textbook forces proof that the Supreme Court declared Secular Humanism a religion. Since it is a religion and since it is taught in the schools, the act of teaching it is unconstitutional, the opposition maintains.

But what is Secular Humanism? In the footnote in the Torcaso case, the Supreme Court cited the case of *Fellowship of Humanity* v. *County of Alameda*.[17] That case contains these two paragraphs:

One of the most respected groups to recognize the humanists as a religious group are the Unitarians. Unitarianism is generally accepted by most authorities as one of the recognized religions. Yet under Unitarian doctrine there is a peaceful coexistence of theists and humanists. A substantial part of the membership and clergy of the Unitarian Church are humanists. In the "Pocket Guide to Unitarianism," edited by Harry B. Scholefield, appears the following (p. 4):

101

"Some Unitarians call themselves 'humanists' and others call themselves 'theists.' The difference between the two groups is not so much a matter for controversy as for mutual understanding and appreciation. The humanist is content, before this life's unanswerable questions, to leave them unanswered. He sees enough in the human scene to demand all his energies of mind and spirit. The fundamental questions seem real enough, but speculation upon them seems hopeless, and all answers proposed must rest upon what William James called 'over-beliefs.' The humanist says in effect, 'One world at a time. I am interested in the world where I am now, in the moral purposes and meanings which the human mind has infused into it, and in the achievement of such ethical goals and ways of life as are possible.' A similar attitude was taken by Buddha."[18]

In the Fellowship of Humanity case, the trial court found that the group met every Sunday at a specified time, that there were some periods of meditation, that the leader read from a newspaper or a magazine or occasionally from the Bible, that the group sang songs, that a speaker spoke on a subject of interest to humanists—such as current political and social issues, and that there was a collection, announcements, and meditation at the end of the service.[19]

In defining the religion of secularism, the *New Catholic Encyclopedia* notes: "Moral judgments can be determined only with respect to specific and developing situations; there cannot exist, therefore, universal norms of conduct, nor do the human values have absolute or permanent significance."[20]

To advance their argument that Secular Humanism is a religion taught in the public schools, the organizations opposed to it point to *Humanist Manifesto I,* issued in 1933, and to *Humanist Manifesto II,* issued in 1973. The opponents of Secular Humanism point out that John Dewey signed the first document and B. F. Skinner signed the second. According to the organizations opposed to the religion, it holds, therefore, that the public schools must be Secular Humanistic since two prominent educators signed the manifestos and since all schools and school teachers allegedly follow the teachings of those two men.

The anti-Secular Humanists distribute copies of *Humanist Manifesto II* to prove that the schools are hotbeds of the religion. The opposition cite portions of the seventeen principles set forth in the second manifesto. Rather than reproduce the entire document, I have chosen to quote a sentence or two from each of the seventeen principles:

1. We believe ... that traditional dogmatic or authoritarian religions that place revelation, God, ritual, or creed above human needs and experience do a disservice to the human species ... As non-theists, we begin with humans not God, nature not deity.

2. Promises of immortal salvation or fear of eternal damnation are both illusory and harmful.

3. We affirm that moral values derive their source from human experience. Ethics is autonomous and situational, needing no theological or ideological sanction.

4. Reason and intelligence are the most effective instruments that humankind possesses.

5. The preciousness and dignity of the individual person is a central humanistic value.

6. In the area of sexuality, we believe that intolerant attitudes, often cultivated by orthodox religions and puritanical cultures, unduly repress sexual conduct. The right to birth control, abortion, and divorce should be recognized.

7. To enhance freedom and dignity, the individual must experience a full range of civil liberties in all societies.

8. We are committed to an open and democratic society.

9. The separation of church and state and the separation of ideology and state are imperatives.

10. Humane societies should evaluate economic systems not by rhetoric or ideology, but by whether or not they increase economic well-being for all individuals and groups,

minimize poverty and hardship, increase the sum of human satisfaction, and enhance the quality of life.

11. The principle of moral equality must be furthered through elimination of all discrimination based upon race, religion, sex, age, or national origin.

12. We deplore the division of humankind on nationalistic grounds.

13. This world community must renounce the resort to violence and force as a method of solving international disputes.

14. The world community must engage in cooperative planning concerning the use of rapidly depleting resources.

15. The problems of economic growth and development can no longer be resolved by one nation alone; they are worldwide in scope.

16. Technology is a vital key to human progress and development . . . We would resist any moves to censor basic scientific research on moral, political, or social grounds.

17. We must expand communication and transportation across frontiers.[21]

Given the two manifestos, the two footnotes in the Supreme Court cases, the removal of prayer and Bible reading from the schools, the development of new courses, and the emphasis on humanizing education, several of the organizations opposed to Secular Humanism have been distributing the following definition of humanism:

Humanism is faith in man instead of faith in God.
Humanism is a "no-God" religion & is as much a religion as Christianity.
Humanism was officially ruled a religion by the U.S. Supreme Court. (The Torcaso case in 1961 and the Seeger case in 1964.)
Humanism promotes: (1.) Situation ethics (also known as relativism) (That is, no absolutes, no right or wrong). (2.) Evolution. (3.) Sexual freedom, including public sex education courses. (Without fixed moral values sex education becomes "how-to" courses.) (4.)

Internationalism. (One worldism, world community, world citizenship, etc.)

Humanism centers on "self" because it recognizes no higher being to which man is responsible. Thus there is much emphasis in public education on each child having a "positive self-concept." The child must see a good picture of himself, to think favorably of himself. This eliminates any need of coming to Christ for forgiveness of sin. It eliminates the Christian attributes of meekness and humility. Where does self-esteem end and arrogance begin? Such terms as self-concept, self-esteem, self-awareness, self-acceptance, self-fulfillment, self-realization, self-understanding, self-actualization, body-awareness, etc. are frequently used. All leave the students occupied primarily with themselves and this is wrong. There are others to consider. Self-centered persons are seldom an asset to themselves, to their friends, family or country. Between the old morality of fixed values and "self-fulfillment" there is a chasm into which many fall. This chasm is "self-indulgence"—a descent to mere animal gratification. How many immature students can bridge this gap of self-indulgence while being taught permissiveness in place of traditional fixed values?[22]

Among the many targets of the anti-humanist forces are these specific courses, programs, and management systems:

anthropology	moral education
behavioral objectives	Program, Planning, Budgeting Systems
black studies	psychology
drug education	sensitivity training
ethnic studies	sex education
humanities	sociology
individualized instruction	values clarification

To help their followers identify programs that are designed by Secular Humanists or humanists, the National Congress for Educational Excellence published a list of nearly three hundred words, phrases, names of programs, and names of professional organizations and foundations that are apparent keys to the religion of Secular Humanism. Here, then, are fifty of the words that would help followers of NCEE and other organizations to identify humanistic programs:

academic freedom	non-verbal expression
acceptance	occult
accountability	open classroom
analysis	parenting
awareness	prescriptive teaching
behavior	problem-solving
body language	programmed instruction
brainstorming	psycho-drama
career education	racism
citizenship	reinforcing
conflict	relativism, scientific
coping	responding
creative writing	secular
democracy	self-analysis
discovery method	self-criticism
emotions	self-understanding
feelings	taxonomy
free schools	transactional analysis
global community	TA for Tots
group discussion	understanding
human growth	values
identity	will of the people
inductive method	witch craft
mastery skills	whole child development
middle schools	world view[23]

In a speech printed in *The Congressional Record* and distributed by The Network of Patriotic Letter Writers, Representative John R. Rarick urged parents to take steps to protect their children from Secular Humanism. His fourth step has been echoed by a number of organizations: "Take your child out of public school as soon as you can. This is the best investment you can make. Why save money to send your children to college if they can't read when they get there!"[24]

Representative Rarick also urged parents to complete a form available from The Network of Patriotic Letter Writers and give it to school officials so that their children would not have to participate in humanistic programs. (Part of the form is reproduced on pages 85–86.) Another writer urges her readers to become acquainted with humanistic terminology and then to study teacher's manuals and course descriptions to determine "if, where or how your children's Christian values are being undermined. Your children's teachers may or may not be following the guides. That's not the point. The teacher is supposed to be following them."[25]

The organizations have been effective; they have attacked the schools on many fronts, demanding that secular humanistic materials and programs be removed from the classrooms and libraries. Frequently the administrators and teachers are taken off guard. They don't fully understand the charge because they do not consider themselves to be members of a religion called Secular Humanism. And many teachers and administrators resent the charge. As one administrator said to me in a telephone conversation: "I've been called many things in my years in the public schools, and I've understood the epithets even though I didn't always like them. But yesterday I was called an evil Secular Humanist who's corrupting youth. Now what in the world am I supposed to be?"

8

THE
TEXTBOOK
ANALYSTS

Norma and Mel Gabler have put "textbooks on trial" in Texas. They have also moved in and out of other states and even other countries with their "ongoing battle to oust objectionable textbooks from public schools."[1] Their influence is not limited by state or national boundaries; their determination to spread the word of their "Christian faith-ministry"[2] has carried them thousands of miles to speak to several hundred thousand people. Their names have become known and respected or feared, revered or scorned, loved or disliked by some people in nearly every state. Their message has been heard: "Acceptable textbooks should be based on high morality, fixed values, Christian concepts, and a proper portrayal of our nation's great heritage."[3]

To accomplish their mission, the Mel Gablers, as they call themselves, have turned their Texas home in Longview into "the nation's largest textbook review clearing house."[4] As the founders of Educational Research Analysts, they "help the 'educationally underprivileged.' As a service organization we are dedicated to HELPING PARENTS who are concerned about what their children are being taught."[5]

In the mimeographed and printed materials made available to concerned parents by Educational Research Analysts, the Gablers make statements like the following:[6] "UNTIL TEXTBOOKS ARE CHANGED, there is no possibility that crime, violence, VD, and abortion rates will do anything but continue to climb. TEXTBOOKS mold NATIONS because textbooks largely determine How a nation votes, WHAT it becomes and WHERE it goes!"

Since they started reviewing textbooks in 1961 and protesting what they consider to be objectionable content, their efforts have paid dividends. For example, in one of the printed sheets they distributed to interested parents in 1977, they noted that "last year God gave parents a number of victories. In Texas alone, the State Textbook Committee did a good job of selecting the best of the available books. Then, the State Commissioner of Education removed 10 books, including the dictionaries with vulgar language and unreasonable definitions."[7]

One year later the Gablers sent this report to their followers: "We submitted 659 pages in our Bills of Particulars against twenty-eight textbooks, including Supplemental Readers, Literatures, and American Histories. All of the Readers and Literature books were either oriented toward violence, cruelty, death and despair, or they were trivial. The history texts were distorted and biased against traditional American values. God saw fit to direct the State Textbook Committee to remove eighteen of these objectionable texts in the first stage. *Many* others should have been eliminated."[8] In that same report, the Gablers noted that the Texas State Board of Education directed the removal of Shirley Jackson's "The Lottery" from three texts and two other stories, "Mateo Falcone" and "A Summer Tragedy" from one text.[9]

When she presents the Gablers' bills of particulars to the Texas State Textbook Committee, Norma Gabler commands the attention of the committee and becomes a source of news stories for the reporters present. An Associated Press reporter filed a news story that contained these first two paragraphs:

Edgar Allen Poe's "gruesome" poem, "The Raven," does not belong in a ninth grade classroom, conservative textbook reviewer Norma Gabler declared Friday.

"You don't need to see television. You can get enough gore and violence in the classroom," she told the State Textbook Committee. "We don't object to Poe as a writer. He does write other things, though."[10]

Mrs. Gabler objected to one history textbook because it "devotes too much space to the Vietnam War, Watergate and farmworker leader Cesar Chavez, while leaving out temperance leader Carry Nation."[11]

The Associated Press reporter wrote that Mrs. Gabler's "complaints ranged from objections to pop art pictures of the Mona Lisa with a mustache to the way a publisher addressed her in written responses." She protested the fact that the publisher referred to her as a Ms. fifteen times even though he knows "I'm an MR-S."[12] Mrs. Gabler becomes the subject of news stories, feature stories, and editorials wherever she goes. Nor is she a prophet without honor in her own community, for she and her husband are frequent subjects of press stories in Longview, Texas. The following paragraph is part of an editorial devoted to the Gablers' specific charges against textbooks submitted for adoption in Texas in 1970:

"Rebels and Regulars" is another very depressing book. As far as the language used, it is in keeping with the characters and plot of the stories, but not the sort of language the thoughtful parent would approve of in his children. There is throughout the book the undercurrent of "a cause," which gives a prejudicial viewpoint, always picturing white man as the villain against different minority groups of individuals.[13]

The *Newport* (Vermont) *Daily Express* devoted editorials to Mrs. Gabler before and after her appearance in that community. In an editorial that summarized her speech and the discussion that followed, the writer included this paragraph:

One individual said that some things in the Bible could be considered offensive. The reply to this was that when immorality was revealed in the Scriptures it was plain to see that it met with God's displeasure and the consequences were disastrous to the individual. In classroom textbooks short term benefits are often emphasized without proper consideration being given to the inevitable unhappy ending.[14]

A reporter for the *Vermont Sunday News* interviewed Mrs. Gabler during her week-long appearance in Burlington to "speak at various public gatherings." The reporter devoted the lead paragraphs to Mrs. Gabler's comments about a fifth-grade history textbook that devoted six pages to Marilyn Monroe and only a few paragraphs to George Washington. In several of her speeches, Mrs. Gabler has noted that she is "not quite ready to have Marilyn Monroe be named Mother of our country." The Vermont reporter wrote: "Mrs. Gabler, an attractive, personable, tactful but firm-minded woman, and her husband started their work many years ago when their son, Jim, who was 16 at the time, asked where he could find the truth if not in the textbooks. Upon reviewing some of the books, the Gablers found so many irrelevant and immaterial topics that they decided someone should perhaps act as sort of a censor and make sure a textbook is, in reality, a textbook."[15]

The Borger (Texas) *News-Herald* devoted 54 column inches to excerpts from the Gablers' bills of particulars submitted to the Texas State Textbook Committee in 1972. The article contained these paragraphs:

Who made it mandatory that a man of such doubtful historical significance as [Cesar] Chavez be included in each history series we examined this year, and at the same time all of them completely censor a truly great man, George Washington Carver?

WHY must such a man be elevated?
Just to mention his name creates respect for him in the minds of students and conceals the fact that his

aim is to do away with the American Free Enterprise System according to an investigation of the California Senate.

In CHALLENGE & CHANGE for high school, we find a heavy emphasis on poverty. Following 17 pages on which poverty is covered, we come to a chapter—an entire chapter—titled, INVESTIGATING POVERTY.—In the United States! Isn't it strange that poverty conditions in the United States are never compared to poverty conditions in other nations?[16]

The (Baltimore) *News American* published a feature story on Norma Gabler after her appearance in Howard County that was sponsored by the Citizens Advocating a Responsible Education. The reporter wrote:

Norma Gabler has been called the greatest watchdog of school books in the United States and the world's busiest textbook reader. She has written articles for major magazines and has been written about in major magazines—recently in U.S. News and World Reports.
She was a central figure in the Kanawha County W. Va. textbook controversy.

Her most serious attack . . . has been directed recently against MACOS, a social studies course titled, "Man—a Course of Study." It became controversial after more than 50 publishers declined its distribution but it was accepted by the National Science Foundation, a federal agency.

According to Mrs. Gabler, the course covers mating with animals, wifeswapping, and survival games. It

112

contains stories of a man consuming his wife and stacking her bones in a heap and of another man cutting off the feet of his living brother.[17]

The Gablers attack on MACOS *(Man: A Course of Study)* has been very successful as well as controversial. The Gabler reviews of MACOS, as reported in The *Burlington* (Vermont) *Free Press,* precipitated responses by a teacher who taught the course and by three anthropologists at the University of Vermont. Excerpts from their letters follow:

This "wife exchange" does not represent "wife swapping." On the contrary, what it represents is the importance of women in Eskimo society, where the woman "takes care of the family's clothing" and "a grown man is helpless if he has no one to make and take care of his clothes." The series never exposes our children to lewd promiscuity or obscenity. As to the stories of marrying animals, what is being referred to are the myths and legends of the Eskimo. Every child who has read Hans Christian Anderson or Grimm's Fairy Tales has been exposed to similar materials. Why should it appear to be so shocking?

The first half of the course contrasts man with animals to help students discern for themselves what makes man human. The second half of the course is about Eskimos. Children compare their culture of today with the Eskimo culture as it existed 50 years ago. Fifth graders are exposed to over 60 lessons throughout the year, each explaining a concept such as animal adaptation, life cycle, social organization of baboons and man (family unit, myths, etc.).

Due to the rather progressive or new approach of Macos it is not hard to understand why a person not familiar with the entire course might misunderstand by taking part of it out of context.

I can safely state that Macos makes no mention of or illusion to any of the following: "Cannibalism," "murder of grandparents," "wife swapping," or "marrying of animals." Such references are ridiculous.[18]

Educational Research Analysts includes copies of the two letters in packets of information sent to concerned parents who want to know more about MACOS. The Gablers have underscored statements with which they disagree, and they have reprinted Mrs. Gabler's letter to the editor of the *Green Mountain Gazette* on the other side of the sheet containing the two letters quoted above. In addition, the Gablers make this comment between the reprint of the two letters: "It is not a question of the books being 'good' or 'bad' because this terminology will depend upon your philosophy. The course is completely acceptable to adherents of the religion of Secular Humanism and completely alien to those who accept absolute values."[19]

The Gablers are greatly concerned about teaching that does not recognize absolute values. For example, Mel Gabler is quoted in the *South Bend Tribune*[20] as having said that "a sentence in a math book, 'There are no absolutes,' is representative of the kinds of damaging statements that cause young people to reject traditional values and follow fads that become popular. He cited drug abuse as one such area that is, in part, a byproduct of this kind of libertine teaching and learning."

Their campaigns against relativism and MACOS have attracted international attention. Mrs. Gabler was invited to spend six weeks in Australia and New Zealand in the summer of 1977 to talk about *Man: A Course of Study*. According to two announcements from Educational Research Analysts, her trip was most successful, as the following paragraph illustrates:

In January 1978 the Premier and his Cabinet removed MACOS (MAN: A COURSE OF STUDY) from *all* Queensland schools, even though it had been stated that Macos was scheduled to go into 5(schools within a year. In February 1978 th SEMP, a substitute program for MACOS designed to incorporate values clarificati(subject. In March 1978 the same Cabinet appoint— committee to make the first thorough investigation of educational aims and direction in over 100 years! The investigation is still in progress. We pray that this search will return Queensland education to basic traditional concepts, because so many Australian youth have been cheated out of useful academic knowledge and skills. Australian businessmen find Oriental and Philippino-educated young people much better qualified than their own Australian youth.[21]

The Gablers have experienced many successes. They have helped to remove textbooks from classrooms throughout the United States as well as in Australia. But it is their work to prepare bills of particulars to present to the Texas State Textbook Committee that resulted in James C. Hefley's writing *Textbooks on Trial*,[22] a book about the Gablers that is in its fifth printing. Hefley tells the story of the Gablers' efforts to clean up textbooks in Texas. His book is now being used as a guide for concerned parent groups throughout the nation.

Mel and Norma Gabler insist that parents who want to protest textbooks must do their homework. A concerned parent who requests a set of reviews receives this advice: "There is MUCH that you as a parent or concerned teacher can do, but you MUST observe some important 'do's' and 'don'ts.' Among them, NEVER protest any textbook until YOU have personally examined the 'questioned' portions in the book (or books) involved. To do this, our reviews can be of great help to you."[23]

In effect, then, the Gablers tell their followers that they do not have to read entire books—only the "questioned" parts. And to find the "questioned" parts, the would-be censors have only to refer to the Gabler-distributed reviews. Several concerned citizens in various communities have, apparently, followed the

Gabler reviews and have underscored the "questioned" parts in textbooks, thus making it appear as if the concerned citizens read the books before protesting them. Another concerned citizen used Gabler-distributed reviews as the basis of a two-hour speech before a school board, protesting specific books. (See page 41.)

The Gablers also give this advice to concerned citizens who are thinking about protesting textbooks: "ALWAYS try to make your case to key area leaders and one or more school board members BEFORE confronting your school or making a public protest. To educators you are an 'outsider' who is 'infringing' in 'their' area when you question, or even examine, school subject matter. Thus, because of professional pride, even good, concerned educators will feel professionally bound to defend what they are using."[24]

The Gablers know that they can expect results when they write bills of particulars on books presented for Texas state adoption which they consider to be offensive. And the Gablers share their bills of particulars with concerned citizens who want to object to specific books. Included in a packet of reviews that one concerned parent received from Educational Research Analysts is a copy of a 27-page letter from the Gablers to the Texas State Commissioner of Education.[25] Dated August 9, 1974, the letter requested the Commissioner not to accept the Ginn 360 Reading Series for use in Texas. The Gablers made 163 objections to ten of the readers for grades seven and eight. In their letter, which they provide to parents who request reviews of the Ginn series, the Gablers cite specific paragraphs and page numbers in the student's or teacher's edition and quote the questionable passage before giving their objections. The following are eleven representative objections grouped according to the titles of the book in the series:

Conflicts. P. 77, Question 3, "What are some other commonplace experiences that cause fear in people? How might people deal with them? Choose one of these experiences and tell how you think you would deal with it." OBJECTION: Invasion of privacy.

P. 128, Question 1, "What is the meaning of long hair to those adults who might object to it? What do you think might be the reason for this? What does long hair mean to you?" OBJECTION: Puts adults in bad light.

Awakenings. P. 67, par. 2, last sent., "School was such a bore." OBJECTION: Depreciates school.

P. 69, par. 6, lines 4–5, "It was so false, so pointless. How could they sing of the land of the free, when there was still racial discrimination." OBJECTION: Majority of people are free. Only people in jail are not free.

P. 78, Poem, "Corners on the Curving Sky," lines 2–5, ". . . that means that you and I can hold completely different points of view and both be right." OBJECTION: No definite standards—situation ethics.

Pp. 81–86, Title, "What Are the Doldrums?" OBJECTION: This story is silly and a waste of time except for pure amusement.

Changes. P. 17, par. 4, line 3, "the day apricots were ripe enough to steal." OBJECTION: Implies that there is nothing wrong with stealing.

P. 48, last par., "But it was always China that we were taught was home. In those days we were all *immigrants.* Whether we were born in America or not, we were all immigrants." OBJECTION: This does not foster partriotism toward America and is somewhat of a derogatory statement about our country.

Failures. P. 19, par. 3, lines 2–3, "Besides Aunt Mo's too dang nosey." OBJECTION: Implies profanity.

Speculations. P. 39, Question 3, "Munro asks, can an instrument have 'second sight' or respond to forces that are beyond our reckoning? What answer would you give? Do you think that the events in this story could happen in real life?" OBJECTION: What does this have to do with literature?

Questions. P. 57, first teacher's note: "The title (Luther) has allusive force, recalling Martin Luther and Martin Luther King, Jr., both reformers." OBJECTION: These two men should not be put in the same category. Martin Luther was a religiously-dedicated, non-violent man.

The Gablers' objections do not go unnoticed in Texas. According to stamped comments[26] on the copy of the 27-page letter of objections, twenty-six of the 183 objections were honored. The 26 objectionable passages or offensive words were deleted or the entire story or poem was replaced in the Texas version of the Ginn series.

Every set of readers—in fact, every textbook—submitted for adoption in Texas is scrutinized as carefully by the Gablers as the Ginn 360 Series. The following are representative objections from the bill of particulars that the Gablers submitted on *Serendipity* and *Diversity,* two books for grades seven and eight in the Houghton-Mifflin reading series:

Serendipity—Teacher's Guide. P. 81, paragraph 2: "Students may wish to discover under what signs of the zodiac they were born and what those signs supposedly tell them about their characters and their futures. Have students take notes . . . and report." OBJECTION: Indoctrination in variations of occult religion.

P. 240, paragraph 1: "Students who enjoy science fiction might like to write an original story . . . in which the earth is taken over by bacteria." OBJECTION: How morbid! Is this helping students learn to read better?

Serendipity—Student's Book. Pp. 32–44: "The Street Kids" Ghetto kids harass an old eccentric watchman of a construction site in New York City. OBJECTION: The names the kids call him are very uncomplimentary and might give 7th graders some new ideas (Weirdo, loony man, Mister Creepsie, creep, Nuts, Kook).

P. 73, col. 1, lines 8–11: "That Quakers were a type of Christian, I also knew—perhaps they were Christians who were particularly honest." OBJECTION: One is either honest or dishonest. This puts Christians in bad light.

P. 114, col. 1, par. 3, lines 1–3: "No animal has been able to mold its life or environment in the way man has done." OBJECTION: Man is NOT an animal.

P. 315, question 9: "What is your reaction to the principle of the game Finders Keepers?" OBJECTION: Implies that one can either accept it or reject it—no moral standard by which to judge the game.[27]

The following are representative objections included in a bill of particulars that the Gablers sent to the Texas Commissioner of Education about two history textbooks submitted by Allyn & Bacon:

The People Make a Nation. Pp. 327–331: Pages of songs. OBJECTION: Is the space for these songs appropriate in a history text? Surely the writing of the Star Spangled Banner, virtually unknown to students today, would have far more historical value and certainly has more historical impact.

Pp. 335–336: "A Drug Addict." OBJECTION: Although the closing paragraph states that drug addiction is ruining our country the overall impact of the article is not only to condone drug taking but to make drugs freely available for everyone. It arouses sympathy for the user rather than encouraging elimination of the use of drugs. Even stealing is justified for a drug addict.

Pp. 352a–352c: INDEX (1.) There are many more listings under blacks than for any other listings. (2.) Poverty is second. (3.) Far behind in 3rd place is "Cities", but note the references: "CITIES: black riots in, 269–271, 279–280; corruption and, 110–113; Great Depression and, 143–147; life of poor children in, 101–102; street cleaning in, 130–131; threat of fire in, 103, women in, 104." OBJECTION TO (1.): Note how many pages are listed for blacks compared to "Indians, American: poverty and, 304–306; Mexican Americans, 298–301; Puerto Ricans, 291–294; No mention of just plain 'Americans.' "

[The Gablers list the Table of Contents.] OBJECTION: An examination of a portion of the table of contents does much to reveal the philosophy of those responsible for this text.

[The Gablers reprint two pages of quotations and questions, with little regard for answers. "Keys" should quotes reveal the heavy emphasis that is placed on questions, with little regard for answers. 'Keys' should unlock, but how can unanswered questions unlock the mind's power. Continuous questions without answers produce frustration. This is a behavioral change method used to condition students to the false idea that there are no basic eternal truths, and can be an instrument for making the student "a puppet on a string."

Teacher's Guide, p. 28: "UNIT I FOUNDERS AND FOREFATHERS: WHO WERE THE PEOPLE WHO MADE AMERICA?"

"The first unit focuses attention on the rich ethnic and racial diversity of the people who made America . . . The larger purpose is to encourage an understanding of the fact that all of these groups have contributed to the building of our society and its institutions. In this sense, *all of our forefathers are founding fathers* whether they framed the laws and constitutions of our early history or whether they recently helped shape important changes in labor relations or in urban educational institutions." [Italics, the Gablers'.] OB-JECTION: This is a complete distortion of history. Why is there such a determination to re-write history? "FOUND-ING FATHERS were statesmen of the Revolutionary War period particularly those men who wrote the Constitution of the United States. The founding fathers included Benjamin Franklin, Alexander Hamilton, James Madison, George Washington, and other delegates to the Constitutional Convention of 1787." P. 372, Volume 6, THE WORLD BOOK ENCYCLOPEDIA.

The People Make a Nation, Volume 1. Pp. 14, 15: "It did not take the upper classes in English society long to realize that the problem of a huge population of poor and desperate people . . ." OBJECTION: What a background to give 14 year old children about the early settler—concentrating on the poor to be able to emphasize class systems.

P. 18: OPINION USED IN PERSUASION. "Write a speech of persuasion in which you use selected details to convince your parents to increase your allowance; to give you permission to stay out late at night; to have friends at home when nobody else is home; to allow you to wear any type of clothing to school." OBJECTION: This is inexcusable!! The questions listed are all matters about which parents already receive too much "convincing." Children need encouragement to uphold rather than break family standards. Why couldn't students be asked to do something to please their parents, something to better themselves, something to help their community—something constructive?

Pp. 34–43: Devoted to slavery and indentured servants. OBJECTION: Why 10 pages and two pictures here, plus nearly an entire chapter later, to emphasize the horrors of slavery which has long been eliminated. This can serve only to arouse racial tensions.

P. 98: Pictures. OBJECTION: In a place of prominence is an endorsement for a radical politician. In the lower lefthand corner is the same picture which appears in most of the history texts offered this year. A picture which conveys a distorted image of town meetings. Worst of all is the clenched fist emblem of a revolutionist.

P. 174: A discussion of gun control. OBJECTION: The text is obviously in favor of gun control which is evident from their quoting a member of the National Rifle Association as favoring. In the eyes of the student this would nullify much of the influence of the NRA which has fought so hard to protect citizen rights.[28]

The Gablers have frequently pointed out the importance of the Texas textbook adoptions. "Our state adoptions have a nationwide effect, since Texas issues the largest contracts for textbooks in America ($40 million this year alone). Because of these large contracts, publishers are willing to make changes requested by the State. For example, Texas adopted books cannot include offensive language—they must be cleaned up or eliminated. Thus, publishers can use as a sales point in other states that their books survived the tough Texas adoption process; and some sell the improved books nationwide to save the expense of printing plates."[29]

Apparently the Gablers feel their campaign against textbooks has been so successful that they can now concentrate on library books and films as well. In one of their recent announcements to concerned parents, they called for reviews of library books. They also called for contributions to help them build a permanent building to enlarge Educational Research Analysts, which has a full-time salaried staff of six plus many unpaid volunteers.

The Gablers are obviously convinced that they know what is best for America's children, and they have the dedication, the drive, and the spirit to achieve their goal. They seem to have hundreds of dedicated followers, too, since the number of censorship incidents in which Gabler-distributed materials are used is on the rise.

A
TIME
TO
ORGANIZE

AASA ACLU AEA AFT ALA ALEC CARE
COFAR CPE CURE GEM IRA LITE NCEE
NCSS NCTE NEA NOW PARENTS PONY-U
SCA TSDAR

Acronyms and initialisms abound in the world of censorship. The twenty-two organizations listed above divide equally into two distinct camps: groups that want to change the curricula of the public schools by removing or altering books and courses; organizations that—among many other activities—oppose censorship. However, they do have at least one thing in common: both groups represent only a tenth—or even less—of the state, local, and national organizations that are involved, in major or minor roles, in the battles over the books.

How many organizations are there? That question is virtually impossible to answer because some local organizations are formed to remove one book from a library or classroom, and they dissolve once the battle is won or lost. Other groups form for the purpose of achieving long-range goals. Still others come and go, expanding or nearly dissolving depending on the times and the issues. But at any given time there are probably no fewer than two hundred organizations—many of which would censor books.

Two hundred may seem like a very large number, but it is probably an extremely conservative estimate. At the time of this writing, there are are at least eight organizations in Indiana alone that would like to eliminate specific books from libraries and schools. That number does not include local and state chapters of national organizations. And it must be remembered that Indiana is not in the top four or five states when it comes to censorship. Therefore, the number of organizations involved in censorship battles may well exceed three hundred. A small percentage of the groups will be mentioned here. It is not my purpose to expose or to praise, to condemn or to applaud. Rather, I will only give as much information as I have obtained about each major group so that the reader can attempt to determine the impact of the organizations on the public schools. Wherever possible, I took the information from an organization's recruiting brochure.

AMERICAN EDUCATION ASSOCIATION. A former principal of Bushwick High School in Brooklyn founded the American Education Association in 1938. Dr. Milo F. McDonald had talked individually to communist teachers in his school about their rights. He informed them that it was "his contention that teachers in the public schools ought to uphold our Constitution. If he or she wished to espouse an alien philosophy, it could be done in a public square under the First Amendment, but not a classroom of tax supported schools." Dr. McDonald brought "the battle out into an open faculty meeting and with the help of teachers who believed as he did, the American Education Association was formed."[1]

In 1968, the AEA and cooperating organizations formed the Joint Committee on Education "to combat the inroads by PEARL (Public Education and Religious Liberty), which group seeks to destroy all Godly religion in education and denies aid to private and parochial schools." The first project of the Joint Committee was "to expose and remove atheistic sex education from the classrooms."[2] The cooperating organizations included: Parents Resisting Invasion of Rights in Training Youth, Parents and Taxpayers, Queens Co. Chapter—Catholic War Vets, National Federation of American Party Women, St. Michael's Forum and Associates, National Traditional Caucus, Parents of New York United, National Coalition for Children, National Congress for Educational Excellence, Concerned Catholic Parents of Greater Cleveland, Citizens United for Responsible Education, and The Mel Gablers—Educational Research Analysts.[3]

Required reading for the Joint Committee included *The National Educator, The School Bell* (a publication of the National Congress for Educational Excellence), the AEA's *Educational Signpost,* textbook reviews distributed by America's Future, and Sister Monica Folzer's *Professor Phonics.*[4] Current concerns of AEA seem to be Secular Humanism, sex education, phonics, a return to the McGuffey Readers, the removal of MACOS *(Man: A Course of Study)* from the schools, the restoration of prayer in the schools; starting with a movement requesting one minute of silent prayer,[5] and opposition to the Equal Rights Amendment.[6]

AMERICA'S FUTURE, INC. "America's Future, Inc. is a non-profit, unendowed educational foundation established in 1946 to help preserve our constitutional form of government and our free-enterprise economic system . . . It operates in the public interest and receives its support solely from contributions except for a small income from sales of books, pamphlets and a fortnightly newsletter."[7] Based in New Rochelle, New York, America's Future supplies reviews of social studies textbooks from a conservative point of view. Using a specific set of criteria, the reviewing committee of sixteen professional educators looks for balanced treatment in textbooks.

"The purpose of the Textbook Evaluation Committee is to evaluate social studies textbooks to determine their accuracy and competence and to report objectively the extent to which they give misleading or false impressions about our American form of government, our unique economy, our history and the relationship of the United States and its citizens to the other countries and peoples of the world. The reviewers will also recommend textbooks which meet the Committee's standards."[8]

AMERICAN LEGISLATIVE EXCHANGE COUNCIL (ALEC). Based in Washington, D.C., ALEC is "committed to curbing the excessive growth and power of government, especially at the federal and state levels." It is also "committed to making government more efficient, more accountable to the people, and more fiscally responsible."[9] ALEC's members are "Democrats, Republicans, and Independents who are dedicated to preserving our individual freedoms, basic American values and institutions, private property rights, our productive free enterprise system, and getting back to limited representative government."[10]

ALEC recommends legislation to be introduced at the state level. It provides legislators with suggested bills each year. The legislation is so edited that a state senator or representative can introduce it without making too many changes. Of the twenty-two suggested pieces of legislation for 1977, five dealt with education. The first bill calls for the establishment of a high school course on the "essentials and benefits of the free enterprise system" which all students "must complete successfully as a prerequisite for graduation."[11]

The suggested parental rights act is designed to protect parents and students from "humanistic education" with its "values oriented" programs. The explanatory statement preceding the bill contains this quotation from Onalee McGraw's *Secular Humanism and the Schools: The Issue Whose Time Has Come,* a publication of The Heritage Foundation: "Humanistic education is the latest manifestation of the so-called progressive life-adjustment philosophy that has dominated our schools and teacher education for decades. Humanistic education places all emphasis on the child's social and psychological growth, instead of on the learning of basic reading, writing, thinking, communicating skills, and factual knowledge."[12]

The parental rights act is designed to protect the family from possible invasions of individual and family privacy through "values-oriented programs that use clinical psychological techniques to probe and mold the social, moral, political,

127

and economic attitudes and values of students and their families
. . . It also establishes parents as the primary authority over
what their children are taught."[13] Finally, "the suggested act
also establishes the right of parents and guardians to review
and correct all student records involving their children."[14]

The suggested teacher proficiency act calls for any superintendent, principal, or teacher applying for certification to pass
proficiency examinations in English and mathematics. The English test would include "grammar, sentence structure, spelling
and phonics, both encoding and decoding."[15]

The suggested school discipline act restores corporal
punishment to the public schools;[16] and the recommended forced
busing prohibition memorial "requests Congress to end forced
school busing and return the authority over public schools to the
people at the local and state level, by approving and submitting
to the states for their ratification on appropriate amendment to
the U.S. Constitution."[17]

THE JOHN BIRCH SOCIETY. Since it was founded in 1958 by Robert
Welch, the John Birch Society has attracted both a great
number of detractors and a large number of members. It currently boasts more than four thousand chapters devoted to fight-
ing Communism, lowering taxes, and battling the Equal Rights
Amendment.[18] According to its founder, the "longrange objective of the Society has been condensed into the slogan: 'Less
government, more responsibility, and—with God's help—a better world.' "[19]

Although Society chapters do not become directly involved
in exerting pressures on school curricula, they have made their
presence known in several textbook battles, including
Kanawha County, West Virginia.[20] The Society's interest in
education manifests itself in a half dozen publications which,
according to a member of the home office, are designed to "combat liberal trends and the declining quality of education." In
addition, the Society distributes reprints of one of its journal
articles, "The N.E.A., Dictatorship of the Educariat," in which
the author makes this charge: "The *real* purpose of the National
Education Association's phony demands for more money, and

the epidemic of decisions declaring the property tax illegal, is to provide a superficially plausible excuse for the federal government to nationalize control of every school, schoolchild, and schoolteacher in America."[21]

COUNCIL ON INTERRACIAL BOOKS FOR CHILDREN. "In 1965, a group of concerned editors, librarians, writers and educators formed a voluntary group—the Council on Interracial Books for Children (CIBC)—to initiate much needed change in the all-white world of children's book publishing and to promote a literature for children that better reflects the aspirations of a multiracial, multicultural society. Much of the improvement in the quality of children's literature since then is a result of the CIBC's consciousness-raising workshops, seminars, conferences and of its publication, the *Bulletin*."[22]

The Council produces a number of film strips and publishes many books—all of which are designed to point out sexism and racism in school and library books. In one of the Council's publications, 235 books "are examined for sexism, racism, materialism, elitism, individualism, conformism, escapism and ageism—as well as for cultural authenticity and effect on the self-image of female and/or minority children. The reviews explore the 'hidden messages' which every author, intentionally or unintentionally, transmits to young people."[23]

Titles of the Council's filmstrips include "Identifying Sexism and Racism in Children's Books," "Unlearning 'Indian' Stereotypes," "From Racism to Pluralism," and "Understanding Institutional Racism." In its announcement of the book, *Stereotypes, Distortions and Omissions in U.S. History Textbooks,* the Council suggests: "Use this content analysis instrument to evaluate new textbooks before deciding which to purchase, or analyze your own textbooks for racism and sexism before starting to teach another term . . . The manual clarifies the subtle ways in which new texts perpetuate stereotypes and distortions."[24]

In cooperation with the Foundation for Change, the Council has established the Racism and Sexism Resource Center for Educators. The Center develops, publishes, and distributes teaching materials to combat sexism and racism; it evaluates textbooks for race and sex bias; it evaluates storybooks for the human—and the anti-human—values they convey to children; and it produces filmstrips and conducts workshops.[25]

THE EAGLE FORUM. Founded by Phyllis Schlafly, the Eagle Forum is dedicated to defeating the Equal Rights Amendment; but it is also concerned with the schools, with the pro-life movement, with equal employment opportunities, with the right of the government to provide for the common defense, and with many other rights.[26]

In the field of education, the Eagle Forum supports the "right of parents to insist that the schools: (a.) permit voluntary prayer; (b.) teach the 'fourth R' (right and wrong) according to the precepts of Holy Scriptures; (c.) use textbooks that do not offend the religious and moral values of the parents; (d.) use textbooks that honor the family, monogamous marriage, woman's role as wife and mother, and man's role as provider and protector; (e.) teach basic educational skills such as reading and arithmetic before time and money are spent on frills; (f.) permit children to attend school in their own neighborhood, (g.) separate the sexes for sex education, gym classes, athletic practice and competition, and academic and vocational classes; if so desired."[27]

Through *The Phyllis Schlafly Report,* Mrs. Schlafly expresses her views on education or has them expressed through others. For example, the entire December 1976 issue was devoted to the late Jo-Ann Abrigg's article, "In the Name of Education." Mrs. Abrigg described the religion of humanism, behaviorism and humanism, behavior modification as used in the schools, and the cry for relevancy in the classroom. Mrs. Abrigg concluded her article with these two paragraphs:

When the Supreme Court took God out of the classroom, the elitist educationists replaced Him with the religion of Humanism. We, the people of America, are the only ones who can protect our children from futuristic manipulation by these elitists.

But we must begin now—we can't wait for the next generation to take action. By then they will have been 'educated' to conform to the new definition of education, and educated to hold allegiance only to man and to a one-world government. They will never even know that they were misled. They may never know America the Beautiful. Above all, they might never know God.[28]

GUARDIANS OF EDUCATION FOR MAINE (GEM). GEM is an "educational research organization staffed by volunteers." Members of GEM believe that the only way "to reverse the trend of declining test scores and to prepare students for productive lives in a free society" is to insist on a curriculum and methodology that stress academic competition, discipline, and traditional subjects. Members of GEM believe in "rugged individualism" not in the "prevailing collective (group) approach to the solving of ethical, intellectual, and social problems." The members believe there is "little relationship between quality education and the amount of money spent on education." Finally, GEM's members believe that "true local control of school can exist *only* when there are *no* federally-funded, i.e., federally-controlled programs."[29]

New members of GEM receive a copy of Onalee McGraw's *Secular Humanism and the Schools: The Issue Whose Time Has Come,* which was published by The Heritage Foundation.[30] In opposing a proposed health education program for Maine schools, GEM distributed a fact sheet that included this statement: "Drug and Alcohol Abuse Education, Sex Education, Family Life Education, Mental Health Education, Values and Death Education have been in American schools for the past fifteen years and have resulted in an increase in the use of alcohol and drugs by teenagers and increased permissiveness in teenage sexual relations and subsequent unwanted pregnancies and student depression."[31]

GEM advertises that it has "documented information on many educational strategies, programs, etc." The flyer listed forty-four topics including: character education, sensitivity training, values clarification, health education, the role of the change agents, social studies, group dynamics, role playing, and special education.[32]

THE HERITAGE FOUNDATION. Joseph Coors, the prominent brewer, established The Heritage Foundation in Washington, D.C., in 1974. It is a "tax-exempt public policy research institution dedicated to the principles of free enterprise, limited government, individual liberty, and a strong national defense. In its four years of existence, Heritage has developed a wide range of services aimed at delivering cogent research to key decisionmakers in the policy arena in a timely fashion, and at better informing the public about the principles on which our nation was founded."[33]

The Heritage Foundation publishes *Education Update,* which presents a specific view of education, as these headlines illustrate:[34] "Religious Freedom: The First Amendment and the Schools—The Battle Lines are Forming," "Indiana: Superior Court Judge Rules Biology Text Unconstitutional," "How School Control Was Wrested from the People," "A Christian School Official Speaks Out," "Values Education: Some Observations," "Special Supplement Enclosed: A Parent's Guide to Textbook Review and Reform by Norma and Mel Gabler."

In a story in which a minister is quoted as saying that Secular Humanism is, indeed, a myth, the editor of *Education Update* writes:

> Many parents, despairing of gaining the illusory 'neutrality' which the Supreme Court has decreed must exist in the public schools, have opted to place their children in non-public schools. Mothers who have taken jobs in order to pay private school tuition will be astounded to learn that all of their sacrifices have been motivated by a desire to 'attack the public schools—their academic freedom and their academic integrity.' It is precisely because too many tax supported schools no longer have any respect for either academic freedom or integrity, however, that parents

in ever increasing numbers are taking concerted action within or without the public school system.[35]

The Heritage Foundation has published two monographs on education by Onalee McGraw, coordinator of the National Coalition for Children which is an organization "dedicated to the preservation of the family and the defense of parental rights in education."[36] The first of Dr. McGraw's monographs is entitled *Secular Humanism and the Schools: The Issue Whose Time Has Come* (See pages 127 and 131). It contains this quotation from Paul A. Kienel, Executive Director of the Western Association of Christian Schools: "The Christian school movement is the fastest growing education movement in the country. The force behind it is that the Christian community is having trouble identifying with the public school system. Academically and morally, it no longer represents their views. If the public schools continue to drop the ball and lose the faith of the American people, we're going to continue to grow."[37]

The second of Dr. McGraw's monographs is entitled *Family Choice in Education: The New Imperative*. It contains these two paragraphs:

All too often the tragic reality of a generation of lost children has been covered up by the carefully-honed public relations skills of the education monopolists. For too long, questions on the essence of education have not been addressed. Too many educators have derailed debate on the vital questions by denouncing any who dared to dissent from their orthodoxy as bigoted reactionaries who merely wish to escape from those of a different race or economic background. Yet, what is apparent to all concerned with the future of children rather than their own self interest is that what really divides families today is not race or class but questions of fundamental human values.[38]

INDIANA EDUCATION COALITION. The apparently newly formed Indiana Education Coalition distributed a list of very short reviews of textbooks in 1978. The books reviewed were those that the State Textbook Adoption Commission had adopted in the English language arts for a five-year period. The Indiana adoption calls for the state to select as many as seven books in each field for each grade; then, local committees composed of teachers and lay members of the community choose one book for each grade or semester-long course. The Indiana Education Coalition sent its reviews to people throughout the state, apparently hoping to influence the selection of books at the local level.

The IEC made this prefatory statement:

> There are many theories and excuses for this admitted decline in our educational system, and we realize there are many situations contributing to this problem. We don't claim to have all the answers. However, we would like to take a look at one area of concern . . . textbooks. Texts present philosophies and values. What kind of character is this knowledge producing? Much theory talks of a positive self-image. Why, then, do we find so much negative self-image, negative morality, and negative Americanism in these books? Why must:
> - running away from home be emphasized and glamourized?
> - students be subjected to an imbalance of crime, divorce, fear and death?
> - teachers, parents and America be downgraded?
> - stories of violence, cruelty and profanity be emphasized?
> - students look at a distorted three legged nude, with an enlarged breast; interpret, analyze, observe, reach a class consensus, and write an individual thesis?
> - right and wrong depend on the situation?[39]

LET'S IMPROVE TODAY'S EDUCATION (LITE). "LITE came about through the desire of concerned citizens (professional people, housewives, scientists, businessmen—of all occupations, of diverse faiths and political affiliation) to provide information not readily available through so-called 'official' sources. The researchers devote countless hours to varied educational problems, in assisting legislators, laymen, and elected or appointed officials who are intimately involved in the educational system."[40]

LITE has newsletters available on these topics, among others: *Man: A Course of Study,* the role of the federal government in education, values, real phonics, individualized instruction, the burden of school taxation, the hidden curriculum, family life education, and humanism in education.[41]

THE NATIONAL CONGRESS FOR EDUCATIONAL EXCELLENCE (NCEE). "The purpose of the National Congress for Educational Excellence is to protect local autonomy of schools, to defend and support parental and family rights, and to promote the teaching of basic academic skills."[42] *The School Bell,* the official publication of NCEE, is published six times a year. In the March-April 1978 issue, the president of NCEE included this statement of NCEE's position in a column on the back-to-basics movement:

Considering the literacy crisis in which we find ourselves, the NCEE requests a redefinition of the purpose of education, included in the education code of the states, to be that which will foster the intellectual development of the child by providing the essential basic skills, reading, writing, computing and proficiency in the use of the English language. By cultivating the use of the mind to seek the systematic knowledge produced through centuries of academic endeavor, and by instilling our heritage. This definition is to expressly exclude the psychological and sociological approach to education commonly termed "the Affective Domain." Such exclusion is to include but not be limited to the following: sensitivity training, magic circles, human development programs, so-

135

cial awareness, self awareness, personal diaries, death education, situation ethics, value judgment, values clarification, moral value alteration, behavior modification or alteration, humanism, values changing curricula or techniques, training in sexual attitudes, the occult, personal and family emotional development, introspective examination of social and cultural aspects of family life.[43] (See pages 85–86.)

PEOPLE OF AMERICA RESPONDING TO EDUCATIONAL NEEDS OF TODAY'S SOCIETY (PARENTS). "PARENTS is an organization that supports academic excellence, parents' rights, local control of schools, private and public schools without federal controls." The organization sends its members occasional newsletters and alerts—mailings containing emergency news with instructions as to what concerned parents can do, such as write or call a legislator about an impending bill. PARENTS' slogan is: "I wondered why SOMEBODY didn't do something; then I realized that I AM SOMEBODY."[44]

In one of the organization's newsletters, Jil Wilson, one of the founders of PARENTS, wrote a report for parents on the parenting programs that are being added to the public schools' curricula. " 'Parenting' curriculum for schools instruct the students in all aspects of parenthood, role playing every conceivable marital joy and sorrow beginning with courtship and ending in divorce, thus teaching students how to be 'good' future parents."[45] In her report on the program, Mrs. Wilson wrote:

What is happening under the title of PARENTING is a *very well planned* and coordinated takeover of the child, body, mind and soul by the State with assistance of well meaning individuals in some cases and with incredible media exposure . . . Under the title of Parenting is going to come sex education, values education, a push for CHILDREN'S RIGHTS and CHILDREN'S ADVOCATES. It has already been suggested that teenagers ought to have the right to divorce their parents if they

136

want to as a lot of teenagers are living with parents they don't really like . . . Morals will be based on values clarification and students will be led away from the religious ties of the family.[46]

PARENTS OF MINNESOTA, INC.

We, the Parents of Minnesota, in order to preserve, protect and uphold the independence of the Family and to secure the blessings of Liberty to ourselves and our posterity, do hereby re-affirm:

That, the Father is the head of the Family, with the Mother at its center.
That, Parents hold directly from their Creator the mission and hence the right to educate their children.
That, life is a gift from God, a gift that includes; physical life, intellectual, and moral life.
That, Parents are their children's advocates, despite artful deception to the contrary.
That, Abortion and Euthanasia are Murder.
That, every child, should be instructed in harmony with religious, moral and traditional values of the Family.

We charge that in the name of education our children are taught Blasphemy, Profanity and Pagan religions, including Demon Worship. Our children's minds have been assaulted with grotesque and violent material, hopelessness and death. Educators have adulterated their students minds with alien philosophies under the guise of Academic Freedom.

We stand opposed to:
The lowering of Academic standards.
The positional change in education from appeal to the intellect to a constant appeal to emotions.

Bussing, for any reason, other than the legitimate transportation of children to their neighborhood school.

Psychological testing without written permission from the parents.

Situation Ethics, commonly called the "New Morality."

Promotion of Pagan Cultures.

Sex role reversal.

The use of Peer Teaching and Group Dynamics.[47]

Janet Egan, Director of Parents of Minnesota, was quoted as having said: "We teach our children what God says is right, and the schools say 'Do what is right for you.' We used to have a code of absolutes. Cheating was wrong, stealing was wrong, lying was wrong. Now it's OK to cheat, and you have to lie to get along with people. Two plus two used to equal four. Now it equals four only if you want it to."[48] Mrs. Egan said "she finds it ironic that some public schools teach about Transcendental Meditation, yoga, the occult, witchcraft and the devil, but will not allow teaching of the Bible. The schools teach humanism, and yet 'humanism has been found to be a religion twice by the Supreme Court.' "[49]

Mrs. Egan was also quoted as having said that feminism is "one of the greatest evils that has beset education because it's making our girls think career-wise. It's changing their ideals. Women who are career-minded become less domestic-minded and can't take orders from a man. A career makes her unhappy, with less time for her husband and family. We can't all be bosses. Somebody has to be submissive."[50] In cooperation with the Association of the 4 W's, Happiness of Womanhood, Inc., and Young Parents Alert, Parents of Minnesota conducted its third annual seminar in September of 1978. The topic of the day-long conference was "Christian Schools: An Issue Whose Time Has Come."[51] Parents of Minnesota prepares book reviews for its members and supplies them with reprints of current articles as well as with newsletters.

PARENTS RIGHTS, INC. Mae Duggan founded Parents Rights in 1967 after debating Madalyn Murray O'Hair in a three-hour radio debate. "She stated that she had collected over $40,000 tax deductible contributions for her atheist suit. I decided then that we, who cherish a God-centered way of life, must defend it in the courts where we would surely get justice . . . Since 1967 Parents Rights has pursued seven cases in defense of family rights in education, but the courts have turned us away without a hearing."[52]

In 1977, Parents Rights and Citizens for Educational Freedom filed lawsuits in both the City of St. Louis and St. Louis County. The suits "charge that the public schools teach a doctrine of 'secular humanism' in the classroom. This doctrine is a kind of 'religion' that is just as illegal under the U.S. Constitution as a sectarian religion, the suits charge. As such, use of tax money for such purposes in the public schools is unconstitutional, and should be halted."[53]

Similar suits had been filed on four previous occasions but had been dismissed. A St. Louis County Circuit Judge dismissed a consolidation of the four suits, ruling that "tax protest lawsuits could apply only to tax assessments, not to tax expenditures. In addition, he said that tax protests could not be filed as class action, i.e., group lawsuits."[54]

There are dozens of other organizations concerned with school and library textbooks, with specific courses, with the presence or absence of any kind of religion in the classroom, and with the schools' taking a firm stand against communism. The following is a list of only 36 organizations or publications that have figured prominently in state, local, or national controversies over books, teaching methods, teaching philosophies, or entire courses and programs:

Allen County Education Information Committee, Inc.,
    Fort Wayne, Indiana
American Association for the Advancement of
    Atheism, San Diego, California

American Christians in Education, Culver City,
California (See page 31.)
American Humanist Association, San Francisco,
California
The Barbara M. Morris Report, Ellicott City,
Maryland
Billy James Hargis' Christian Crusade, Tulsa,
Oklahoma
Christian Anti-Communism Crusade, Long Beach,
California
Citizens Coalition, Albany, New York
The Citizens Committee of California, Inc., Fullerton,
California
Citizens Committee on Education, Pinellas County,
Florida (See page 54.)
Citizens United for Responsible Education,
Montgomery County, Maryland
Citizens United for Responsible Education,
Montgomery County, Pennsylvania
Committee for Positive Education, Youngstown, Ohio
Concerned Citizens of Elkader, Iowa (See page 41.)
Concerned Citizens and Taxpayers for Decent School
Books, East Baton Rouge, Louisiana (See page
39.)
Concerned Citizens of Middleton Valley, Middletown,
Maryland (See page 56.)
Concerned Parents of Monticello, Iowa (See page 42.)
Concerned Parents and Taxpayers for Better
Education, Nashua, New Hampshire (See page
62.)
Daughters of the American Revolution
Fair Education Foundation, Inc., Clermont, Florida
Frederick County Civic Federation, Frederick,
Maryland

Freedom from Religion Foundation, Madison,
Wisconsin

Humanist Quest for Truth, Brighton, Colorado

Indiana Home Circle, Bloomington, Indiana

Interfaith Committee Against Blasphemy, Wyoming,
Michigan (See page 53.)

The National Educator, Fullerton, California

National Organization for Women (See pages 69 and
81.)

The Network of Patriotic Letter Writers, Pasadena,
California (See pages 96 and 107.)

Parents of New York—United (PONY-U), Clarence,
New York (See pages 60 and 126.)

Parents Who Care, Chevy Chase, Maryland

People Who Care, Warsaw, Indiana (See page 13.)

Reading Reform Foundation, Scottsdale, Arizona

Santa Clara County Citizens Action Committee
Opposing Family Life Education, San Jose,
California

The Society of Evangelical Agnostics, Fresno,
California

Texas Society of the Daughters of the American
Revolution

Young Parents Alert, Lake Elmo, Minnesota. (See
pages 98 and 138.)

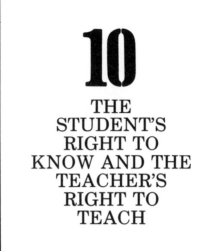

10

THE STUDENT'S RIGHT TO KNOW AND THE TEACHER'S RIGHT TO TEACH

Elementary and secondary school teachers should not enjoy academic freedom because they teach captive audiences. That's what the founder of PARENTS (People of America Responding to Educational Needs of Today's Society) said in a radio broadcast over a Wisconsin statewide network.[1] To support her contention, she said that a federal judge had declared that classroom teachers are not always sufficiently trained nor intelligent enough to merit academic freedom.[2] She then thanked the American Civil Liberties Union for reprinting a paragraph from the judge's opinion in its handbook entitled *The Rights of Teachers.*[3] The founder of PARENTS was obviously referring to these three sentences in the judge's opinion: "The faculty [of a secondary school] does not have the independent traditions, the broad discretion as to teaching methods, nor usually the intellectual qualifications, of university professors. Among secondary school teachers there are often many persons with little experience. Some teachers and most students have limited intellectual and emotional maturity."[4]

In the case of *Mailloux* v. *Kiley,* the judge also said: "Most parents, students, school boards, and members of the community usually expect the secondary school to concentrate on transmitting basic information, teaching 'the best that is known and thought in the world,' training by established techniques, and, to some extent at least, indoctrinating in the *mores* of the surrounding society."[5] The judge further noted that secondary schools are not "open forums in which mature adults, already habituated to social restraints, exchange ideas on a level of parity."[6] The judge expressed his opinion that "it cannot be accepted as a premise that the student is voluntarily in the classroom and willing to be exposed to a teaching method which, though reasonable, is not approved by the school authorities or by the weight of professional opinion."[7]

The teaching method the judge referred to was an English teacher's writing the word *fuck* on a chalkboard in a class discussion of taboo words. After a student defined the word as meaning "sexual intercourse," the teacher noted that society accepts that phrase but does not accept the taboo word he had written on the board. The discussion of taboo words was prompted by student responses to a situation in a novel the class was reading. The students had remarked that a parental protest over the seating of boys and girls together in a one-room schoolhouse was ridiculous. The teacher then departed from the novel to a discussion of taboo words to point out other equally ridiculous objections. Neither the word *fuck* nor the subject of taboo words appeared in the novel under discussion.[8]

Before making its decision, the court called upon expert witnesses to comment on the teaching method involved. The college professors appearing before the court endorsed the method; however, several high school principals and the chairperson of Mailloux's own department "testified that in their opinions it was inappropriate to use the particular word in question."[9] The court recognized the teacher's right to academic freedom as described in several court cases, but it felt that Mailloux had used a teaching method that would not be approved by the teaching profession as a whole. However, the court held that the "attempted dismissal of Mailloux violated the constitutional procedural right recognized by *Keefe* and

143

Parducci—the right of a teacher not to be dismissed for using a 'reasonable' teaching method unless he or she has been put on notice not to use that method."[10]

Citing the *Mailloux* decision, among others, Professor Stephen R. Goldstein wrote an article for a law journal in which he challenged academic freedom for secondary school teachers. Professor Goldstein wrote that "cases involving restrictions on teachers' rights of curricular control are often erroneously viewed as censorship cases when the real issue is who should make curricular choices given the fact that someone has to make choices. With regard to this issue, the arguments that the Constitution allocates curricular decision making authority to the teacher are not persuasive."[11]

Professor Goldstein rejected both professionalism and the First Amendment as arguments in behalf of public school teachers. In refuting the First Amendment argument, Professor Goldstein wrote: "The freedom of expression justification for teacher control is premised on an analytical model of education which views school as a market place of ideas. There is no historical or precedential basis, however, for concluding that the market place of ideas model is constitutionally compelled over the traditional value inculcation model. Thus, in the final analysis, teachers' constitutional rights, in and out of the classroom, do not extend beyond the first amendment rights of all citizens."[12]

Professor Goldstein's conclusions are certain to become popular with the organizations that would censor classroom materials and score specific teaching methods. But before they rely too heavily on the Goldstein argument, the organizations should read Judge Richard P. Matsch's opinion in the case of *Bob Cary, et al.* v. *Board of Education of the Adams-Arapahoe School District.*[13]

The attorneys for the defendant school board members in that case used the Goldstein argument to justify their clients' actions. In a regularly scheduled public meeting, the school board approved 1275 textbooks for use in the high school but disapproved the following ten books: *A Clockwork Orange* by Anthony Burgess; *The Exorcist* by William P. Blatty; *The Reincarnation of*

Peter Proud by Max Ehrlich; *New American Poetry 1945–1960* by Donald Allen; *Starting from San Francisco* by Lawrence Ferlinghetti; *The Yage Letters* by William Burroughs and Allen Ginsberg; *Coney Island of the Mind* by Lawrence Ferlinghetti; *Kaddish and Other Poems, 1958–1960* by Allen Ginsberg; *Lunch Poems* by Frank O'Hara; *Rosemary's Baby* by Ira Levin.[14]

The plaintiff teachers had included the books in their reading lists for their courses. The board did not order the books removed from school libraries; nor did it condemn the books as being legally obscene. Rather, on January 13, 1976, the school board issued a memorandum directing that the ten books "will not be purchased, nor used for class assignment, nor will an individual be given credit for reading any of these books."[15]

In noting that secondary school teachers must have the right of academic freedom, Judge Matsch wrote: "To restrict the opportunity for involvement in an open forum for the free exchange of ideas would not only foster an unacceptable elitism, it would also fail to complete the development of those not going on to college, contrary to our constitutional commitment to equal opportunity. Effective citizenship in a participatory democracy must not be dependent upon advancement toward college degrees. Consequently, it would be inappropriate to conclude that academic freedom is required only in the colleges and universities."[16]

Judge Matsch added that the "Aurora school board has shown its commitment to providing its upper-level students with an opportunity to engage actively in the free exchange of ideas. Specifically, the fact that the courses here are offered as electives indicates the board's recognition that the students have already been initiated into the basics and are prepared to participate critically and creatively. I do not hold that a school board has any obligation to create an open environment in any school. It is enough to conclude that having granted both teachers and students the freedom to explore contemporary literature in these high school classes, the school board may not now impose its value judgments on the literature they choose to consider."[17]

145

In refuting the Goldstein argument, Judge Matsch pointed out that he could not accept the proposition that teachers are, "essentially, extensions of their employers."[18] If teachers must follow only the wishes of the majority as reflected by the school board and school authorities and serve as role models for those authorities, the result would be tyranny. "The tyranny of the majority is as contrary to the fundamental principles of the Constitution as the authoritarianism of an autocracy."[19]

But despite his contention that teachers enjoy academic freedom, Judge Matsch awarded the decision to the defendant school board because he said that the teachers had bargained away their rights to academic freedom with a specific clause in their master contract. Otherwise, the "selection of the subject books as material for these elective courses in these grades is clearly within the protected area recognized as academic freedom."[20] The judge also wrote that the school board's action to prohibit the use of "any material not included in the list of 1275 books" without the teachers' first obtaining approval of school officials "is the kind of broad prior restraint which is particularly offensive to First Amendment freedom."[21] The *Cary* case has been appealed to the Tenth Circuit Court of Appeals on the grounds that individual teachers cannot have their rights to academic freedom bargained away by others.

The Supreme Court has yet to hear a case involving academic freedom in the public schools; however, the lower federal courts have begun to recognize, as in the *Cary* case, the need for academic freedom in the high schools. Two cases—*Keefe* v. *Geanakos*[22] and *Parducci* v. *Rutland*[23]—are particularly significant. In *Keefe,* a teacher was dismissed for having assigned students to read an article containing the word *motherfucker* and for not agreeing to refrain from discussing the word in class again. The English teacher had conducted class discussion of Robert J. Lifton's "The Young and the Old," an *Atlantic Monthly* article about dissent, protest, radicalism, and revolt. Before assigning the article for students to read, the teacher gave students the option of an alternate assignment. He then discussed both the article and the word, explaining the word's origin and telling why he thought the author had used the word. When the school committee requested that the teacher never discuss the word in class again, he refused. The school committee suspended the teacher and instituted dismissal proceedings. The court concluded that the principles of academic freedom embodied in the Constitution barred the teacher's dismissal. In its decision, the court included this quotation from the Supreme Court case of *Wieman* v. *Updegraff:*[24] "Such unwarranted inhibition upon the free spirit of teachers affects not only those who . . . are immediately before the Court. It has an unmistakable tendency to chill that free play of the spirit which all teachers ought especially to cultivate and practice."

In *Parducci,* a high school teacher of English was dismissed as being insubordinate when she refused to comply with her superiors' order that she never again teach Kurt Vonnegut's short story, "Welcome to the Monkey House." Two of the administrators in the school district called the story "literary garbage," and they claimed that its "philosophy" favored "killing off of old people and free sex."[25] They also told the teacher that three students had asked to be excused from the assignment and that several parents had complained about the story. When the teacher did not follow the administrators' orders, the school board dismissed her on the grounds that the story had a "disruptive" effect on the school and that she had refused "counseling and advice of the school principal" and was therefore guilty of "insubordination."[26]

The court upheld the teacher's right to teach the story and denied the school board the right to dismiss her. The court found that the story was appropriate for high school juniors and that it was not obscene. The court also noted that Vonnegut was not advocating the killing of the elderly but that he was satirizing the depersonalization of man in society.[27] In *Parducci,* the court partially answered the question—Should school officials have the power to decide what should be taught and what should be banned?—by declaring that the Vonnegut story, as judged by other works that the students read in and out of school, was not obscene. The court also found that the assignment of the short

147

story was not disruptive to the school; in fact, it was met with apathy by most of the students, except the three who asked to be excused from the assignment.[28]

In *Parducci,* the court applied the so-called *Tinker* test to decide whether or not the assignment of the Vonnegut story was disruptive to the school. In *Tinker* v. *Des Moines Independent Community School District,*[29] the Supreme Court decided that three students could not be suspended from school for wearing black armbands in protest of the Vietnam War. The Court noted that the peaceful protest was not disruptive to the normal operation of the school. In that decision which scholars call a landmark for both student and teacher rights, the Court made this frequently quoted statement: "It can hardly be argued that either students or teachers shed their constitutional rights to freedom of speech or expression at the school house gate."

In the case of *Sterzing* v. *Fort Bend Independent School District,*[30] the court held that "the freedom of speech of a teacher and a citizen of the United States must not be so lightly regarded that he stands in jeopardy of dismissal for raising controversial issues in an eager but disciplined classroom."[31] The court declared that "it is the binding duty of an administrative body to act with full information, with reason and deliberation, and with full benefit of the views of supervisors, principals and others familiar with the curriculum and teaching techniques in the schools, before denying a teacher his livelihood and professional status. It is entirely unfitting that such a board should be swayed by the hearsay remarks of persons not in possession of the facts, without specifically warning the accused of the contemplated action and allowing him a fair and impartial hearing before they act."[32]

The courts have obviously not always decided in favor of teachers and their claim to academic freedom—particularly when the teachers have departed from their assigned subject matter or have used unacceptable teaching methods. For example, the courts have decided that a teacher could not discuss sex in an all-male speech class,[33] that a teacher could not discuss politics in an economics class,[34] that a teacher could not discuss his disapproval of ROTC in an algebra class,[35] and that teachers have no constitutional rights to use unorthodox teaching methods.[36]

The courts do not always decide a case involving academic freedom on that ground alone. For example, a nontenured teacher of English[37] claimed that his First Amendment rights have been violated because he was not rehired "allegedly for assigning *Brave New World* to his class. Although the district court ruled against the teacher on this issue, the Fourth Circuit expressly disavowed this ground in affirming the lower court decision. Instead . . . it based its decision solely on the teacher's nontenured status."[38]

As the aforementioned court cases illustrate, underlying questions—not always openly asked or answered—pervade most cases involving textbooks and library books in the public schools. Does the school board or school committee, as it is sometimes called, have the ultimate authority in the selection and rejection of books and teaching materials? Must the school board or school committee sanction every book, every teaching method, every film used in the schools? Can a book be removed from a classroom or library simply because it offends the sensibilities of some members of the community? Does the student have the right to read and the right to know?

Those are difficult questions that some courts seem reluctant to answer. For the most part, the courts do not want "to involve themselves in the debate over educational purposes and practices, and thus often defer to school board expertise."[39] When the courts do become involved in disputes over textbooks and library books, the answers to the difficult questions sometimes conflict with answers given in different courts, as the following cases illustrate.

Piri Thomas's *Down These Mean Streets* is a graphic, autobiographical account of life in New York's Spanish Harlem. In his attempt to capture the realities of life there, the author uses taboo phrases. The life portrayed in Harlem is not pleasant in this powerful and provocative book that provoked a group of parents in New York's School District 25. In 1971, the parents called the book obscene and asked the District Board to have it removed from the shelves of several school libraries.[40]

149

Responding to the parental request, the board conducted a public meeting in which "all but two of 73 speakers favored retention of the book, either on literary or educational grounds. Nonetheless the Board voted 5–3 to remove all copies of the book from junior high school libraries in the district. The district superintendent promptly complied with the Board's order. About six weeks later, the Board held another public meeting at which the order was modified; copies of the book were to be kept in the libraries which originally bought them, and loaned on request to parents of children attending the school but not to the students themselves."[41]

When a group of parents, teachers, students, and a school librarian brought suit in the United States District Court for the Eastern District of New York, the district court dismissed the complaint without a hearing. Finding no constitutional violation in the court's action, the Court of Appeals of the Second Circuit unanimously affirmed the dismissal. The court noted that some authorized group must determine what a library collection will be. It also observed that shouts of book burning could hardly elevate an "intramural strife to first amendment constitutional proportions." Otherwise, "there would be a constant intrusion of the judiciary into the internal affairs of the school."[42]

The Supreme Court refused to review the case of *President's Council, District 25* v. *Community School Bd. No 25*.[43] However, in a dissenting opinion, Justice William O. Douglas wrote: "What else can the School Board now decide it does not like? How else will its sensibilities be offended? Are we sending children to school to be educated by the norms of the School Board or are we educating our youth to shed the prejudices of the past, to explore all forms of thought, and to find solutions to our worlds's problems?"[44]

President's Council does not answer the difficult questions since the court chose to treat the issue as a matter of shelving and unshelving books that did not involve the curtailment of constitutional rights. In his analysis of the decision, Professor Robert M. O'Neil observed that the "insensitivity of the Second Circuit's disposition . . . is understandable . . . because the case was one of first impression. The simple fact is that no constitutional decisions have defined the relative rights and responsibilities of public libraries and their patrons."[45] Professor O'Neil concluded in his law journal article: "If the citizenry is to be fully informed and if the primary functions of government are to be exercised by a responsible and knowledgeable electorate, then the libraries should be as unfettered as the press, the broadcast media, and the universities."[46]

Five years after *President's Council*, the Sixth Circuit decided that a school board could not remove two books from a school library. In *Minarcini* v. *Strongsville City School District*,[47] the court ordered the school board to return Kurt Vonnegut's *Cat's Cradle* and Joseph Heller's *Catch-22* to the school library. The court observed:

A library is a storehouse of knowledge. When created for a public school it is an important privilege created by the state for the benefit of students in the school. That privilege is not subject to being withdrawn by succeeding school boards whose members might desire to "winnow" the library for books the contents of which occasioned their displeasure or disapproval.[48]

In its decision, the Sixth Circuit Court referred to the lower court's opinion that the school board had not violated First Amendment rights when it removed two books from the school library. The Circuit Court noted: "The lower court in the instant case appears to have read this decision [*President's Council*] as upholding an absolute right on the part of the school board to remove from the library and presumably to destroy any books it regarded unfavorably without concern for the First Amendment. This court does not read the Second Circuit opinion so broadly."[49]

The Sixth Circuit Court observed:

The court must conclude that the board removed the books because it found them objectionable in content and because it felt it had the power, unfettered by the

151

First Amendment, to censor the school library for subject matter that the board members found distasteful
... A public school library is a valuable adjunct to classroom discussion. If a teacher considered Joseph Heller's "Catch 22" to be an important American novel, no one would dispute that the First Amendment's protection of academic freedom would protect both his right to say so in class and his student's right to hear him and to find and read the book. Obviously, the students' success in this last endeavor would be greatly hindered by the fact that the book had been removed from the school library. The removal of books from a school library is a much more serious burden upon freedom of classroom discussion that the action found unconstitutional in *Tinker* v. *Des Moines Independent Community School District*, 393 U.S. 503 (1969). This burden is not minimized by the availability of the disputed book in sources outside the school.[50]

The court noted that it was concerned with the "right of students to receive information that they and their teachers desire them to have." The court added that recent Supreme Court opinions firmly establish "both the First Amendment right to know involved in this case and the standing of the students to raise the issue."[51]

In *Minarcini,* five high school students filed suit through their parents as next friends. The suit challenged the school board's right to determine what books could be selected as textbooks, what books could be selected for the school library, which books could be removed from the school library, and which books could be banned from the high school classroom. The Sixth Circuit upheld the school board's rights to decide which books could be approved as textbooks, but it denied the school board the right to remove previously purchased library books.

Likewise, Judge Joseph Tauro in the United States District

Court in the District of Massachusetts denied a school committee the right to remove an anthology of prose and poetry from the library. The school committee had objected to *Male and Female Under 18* because it contains a poem entitled "The City to a Young Girl." When a parent complained to the chairman of the school committee about the poem, the chairman determined that the book should be removed from the library "without reading any other part of the anthology. The only person he consulted was the complaining parent."[52] Then the chairman called an emergency meeting of the committee "to consider the subject of 'objectionable, salacious and obscene material being made available in books in the High School Library.' "[53] The chairman, who is the owner and publisher of the *Chelsea Record,* also wrote an editorial for his newspaper that evening and published it the next day. The editorial contained these paragraphs:

I think it can be said without contradiction that I am certainly no prude in a certain matters—but the complaint of a father made to me yesterday about passages in a book his daughter obtained at the high school library has almost made me sick to my stomach to think that such a book could be obtained in any school—let alone one here in Chelsea.

I want to bring this matter to the attention of our Administrators and I want to make certain that no such filth will be distributed in our schools.

Quite frankly, more than that, I want a complaint review of how it was possible for such garbage to even get on bookshelves where 14 year old high school—ninth graders—could obtain them.[54]

"The City to a Young Girl" is a poem by a 15-year-old girl who describes how she feels when men look at her on the street. She uses "street language" to refer to parts of her anatomy, and she concludes the poem with these three lines: I swat them off like flies/ but they keep coming back./ I'm a good piece of meat.[55]

Superintendent Vincent McGee stated that it was inappropriate to handle the complaint of one parent in an open school meeting; and he said that Andrew P. Quigley, the owner of the newspaper and chairman of the school committee, was "setting in motion a chain of events that might lead to censorship." Mr. Quigley's response to the superintendent's statement was an editorial in the *Chelsea Record* entitled "Mr. McGee's Censorship." The editorial characterized the poem as "obviously obscene," "filthy," and "vile and offensive garbage."[56]

Throughout his opinion, Judge Tauro quotes from editorials in the *Chelsea Record*. For example, after the editor learned that teachers had filed suit as the result of the removal of *Male and Female Under 18:* "Who needs employees like that? Who needs employees that will fight to keep the kind of tasteless, filthy trash that is contained in this poem we voted to remove? I may even call a special meeting to discuss what we'll do with these insubordinate teachers."[57]

When the editor received a complaint about another book, the owner of the newspaper wrote an editorial condemning *Growing Up Puerto Rican* and the teacher who used the book in an adolescent literature course. The editor called the use of the book "an absolute outrage." The editorial concluded: "Such instances of this type of 'filth' MUST NOT—CANNOT—AND WILL NOT be permitted in Chelsea Schools."[58]

Judge Tauro ordered the book returned to the library. In his conclusion, he wrote:

> The library is "a mighty resource in the marketplace of ideas." *Minarcini* v. *Strongsville City School District, supra* at 582. There a student can literally explore the unknown, and discover areas of interest and thought not covered by the prescribed curriculum. The student who discovers the magic of the library is on the way to a life-long experience of self-education and enrichment. The student learns that a library is a place to test or expand upon ideas presented to him, in or out of the classroom. The most effective antidote to the poison of mindless orthodoxy is ready access to a broad

sweep of ideas and philosophies. There is no danger in such exposure. The danger is in mind control.[59]

There is no doubt that the First Amendment embraces the student's right to know and the teacher's right to teach. The courts have not yet answered all of the critical questions pertaining to those rights, but decisions in a variety of pending cases in federal courts throughout the nation may sharpen the focus on First Amendment freedoms in the classroom.

11

PROTECTING
THE RIGHTS
OF STUDENTS
AND
TEACHERS

A member of the school board removed four books from a high school library in Asheville, North Carolina; then she sent the principal a check to cover the cost of the books. Before demanding that all materials containing objectionable words be removed from the school library, the board member confiscated *The Catcher in the Rye, Of Mice and Men, Andersonville,* and *The Learning Tree.*[1]

The principal ordered a chapter on human reproduction removed from a physiology textbook used in classes in Griswold (Connecticut) High School. The school superintendent supported the action, saying that the censorship protected the students from "lurid pictures" and "subject matter beyond their sensibilities." The objectionable chapter included illustrations of the human reproductive organs. The chapter was removed without the knowledge of the school board, the faculty, the students, or their parents.[2]

Black students staged a week-long boycott of school in Boynton, Oklahoma, after school officials tried to prevent one student from reciting Martin Luther King Jr.'s "I Have a Dream" in a speech contest. The school superintendent said he tried to discourage the student from reading the speech because it contains "racial overtones" that "could have caused some problems." The students returned to school after school administrators said they would allow the recitation of the widely published, highly acclaimed speech.[3]

The National Organization for Women charged that *The Dog Next Door and Other Stories,* a second-grade reader, is riddled with sexism. As a result, the school board of Montgomery County (Maryland) voted not to purchase more copies of the book or have existing copies rebound.[4]

A minister who is also a member of the school board called *Drums Along the Mohawk* "obscene" because it contains the words *damn* and *hell.* The school board of Coffee County (Tennessee) unanimously approved the removal of the book from an assigned reading list.[5]

Library materials showing women in demeaning roles are under scrutiny in the Salisbury school district (near Allentown, Pennsylvania). Asked what standards librarians were using to remove biased books from the library, the chairperson of a school board committee said that books "not in keeping with the times" were unacceptable. Praising the judgment of the librarians, the school superintendent said that he had removed a book from the library after a parent complained about vulgar words in it.[6]

Responding to a group of black parents who complained that *The Adventures of Huckleberry Finn* contains racially derogatory remarks, the school board voted to remove it from required lists at New Trier High School (Winnetka, Illinois).[7]

The Multi-Cultural Non-Sexist Advisory Committee of Cedar Rapids (Iowa) recommended permanent removal of more than one hundred books from the Kenwood Elementary School library. The books were deemed "discriminatory"—racist, sexist, or biased against handicapped people. The Iowa Civil Liberties Union has urged the school board not to bar the books from the library.

The director of the ICLU declared: "Our schools, of all places, should be the last to deal with bad ideas by sweeping them under the rug. If any of these books have in them archaic concepts or bad ideas, they should be singled out for criticism in classroom discussion, not hidden away. These books are a reflection of a society which has been and continues to be racist and sexist in many subtle and not-so-subtle ways. The problem is not cured by removing books from the library."[8]

After one parent complained about *Manchild in the Promised Land,* administrators in the Waukesha (Wisconsin) school system removed the book from the high school library.[9]

The Butler (Pennsylvania) school board voted first to burn and then only to ban *Contemporary American Short Stories,* an anthology that includes works by James Baldwin, Ralph Ellison, Philip Roth, and John Updike. The board responded to a protest by one parent who objected to several sentences in Ellison's "The Battle Royal," which is the first chapter in his novel, *The Invisible Man.*[10]

The Randolph (New York) school board removed nearly 150 books from the high school library in "an attempt to quell complaints of a parent group that wants more say in determining educational policy." The board had the books locked in a safe until a screening committee could decide which books are "fit" reading material for students. Among the authors whose books were removed are Maya Angelou, Isaac Asimov, James Baldwin, Ralph Ellison, Ann Fairbairn, Robert Heinlein, Nat Hentoff, Hermann Hesse, Bernard Malamud, John Neufield, Alvin Toffler, Kurt Vonnegut, Richard Wright, and Paul Zindel.[11]

Calling themselves the "Save Our Children" slate, four candidates for the Trenton (New Jersey) school board prepared to distribute twenty thousand copies of "salacious" excerpts from *Go Ask Alice* in a door-to-door campaign. The candidates said they were running on the issue of "dirty books" in school libraries. Even before the election, the candidates succeeded in having *Go Ask Alice* removed from a middle school library.[12]

Those incidents underscore the vulnerability of many public schools. It is ironic that in a democracy one person or one group—no matter how small—can exert sufficient pressure on some school officials to have books removed from school libraries or classrooms despite the wishes of a majority. But the individual or the pressure group may realize that success is within reach since a majority of the people in a community may be so apathetic about their schools that they will not rise in defense of a book, of a specific course, or of the principle of academic freedom. It is sad to note that an individual or a group can sometimes succeed in having a book or course removed from a school even though the complainants have not read the book or examined the course. It is painful to note that the sensibilities of a few sometimes serve as the guidelines for the masses. No matter how unfortunate, it is true; for in censorship incident after censorship incident described in this book, an individual or a group has influenced the education of many children and has denied them access to information—thus depriving them of the rights to read and to know.

All people in a democratic society have the right to be heard. All have the right to complain. In fact, parents should be concerned enough about their children's education to complain if they believe that something is wrong. But the complaint of a single parent or of a single group should not serve as the basis for action by a school board or by school officials. Rather, the handling of that complaint should be part of a set of specific procedures in which all parties involved—the teacher or librarian, school administrators, school board, and book reviewing committee—examine the problem carefully before any action is taken.

No person in a school corporation should be empowered to act alone in a censorship incident, but too often that is the case.

One teacher, or one librarian, or one school administrator hears one complaint from one parent and removes a book from a library or classroom. That should never occur in a democratic society, and it could not occur if every school in the United States had an established set of procedures for handling complaints about books, courses, teaching materials, and teaching methods. But the fact is—and many censors know this—that relatively few schools have official policies and procedures for handling complaints despite the fact that model policies are available from many professional educational organizations. The following organizations, among others, can supply sets of procedures for handling complaints as well as other helpful information in dealing with censorship problems:

American Association of School Administrators
1801 North Moore
Arlington, VA 22209

American Federation of Teachers
11 Dupont Circle
Washington, DC 20036

International Reading Association
800 Barksdale Road
Newark, DE 19711

National Council for the Social Studies
Suite 406, 2030 M Street, NW
Washington, DC 20036

National Council of Teachers of English
1111 Kenyon Road
Urbana, IL 61801

National Education Association
1201 16th Street, NW
Washington, DC 20036

Office for Intellectual Freedom
American Library Association
50 East Huron Street
Chicago, IL 60611

Speech Communication Association
5205 Leesburg Pike
Falls Church, VA 22041

In addition to a set of procedures for handling complaints, every school system should have a materials selection policy that is readily available to all citizens who wish to have a copy. The departments in the secondary schools should have statements of philosophy about their programs available to all concerned citizens, and the departments should have specific objectives for their courses. They should also be ready to explain, orally or in writing, how specific textbooks and supplementary readings help to meet those objectives.

Perhaps one reason that the schools are so vulnerable to attacks from the censors—in addition to the fact that not all of them have the aforementioned policies and procedures—is that the schools have not always communicated effectively with students, parents, and other members of the community. The schools need to do a far better job of explaining what they teach, why they have chosen specific teaching materials, and how those materials meet the objectives of the courses. In more than one instance, the censors have indicated that they were not given such information or that they were "put down" when they asked for it. A negative, condescending, or inadequate response to a question will only spur the censors on to continued action.

Another major reason that the schools are vulnerable is that too much of the censorship of school materials starts from within the system or too much is quickly accepted by one or more school people who ignore the procedures for handling complaints—if the system has one. School people who are prone to censor teaching materials must realize that they, too, are guardians of academic freedom and the student's right to know. And members of the school board must recognize that they may have the right to approve textbooks and the school curriculum but that they must be aware of recent court decisions before they act in haste.

In far too many incidents of censorship, school officials have attempted to "keep the matter quiet." That strategy may well backfire. Censors are willing to exert a great deal of pressure because they know that some school officials will respond favorably in fear that they might otherwise receive negative publicity. On the other hand, few censors are willing to be exposed. They do not always want their objections made known to the public. They do not want to run the risk of ridicule and scorn if the general public opposes what they stand for. And in many instances the general public would oppose the censors if they only knew what the censors were after.

Textbook publishers have also tended to remain quiet on the subject of censorship. Several wrote to me that they had experienced no censorship problems; a few of them were the subjects of bitter bills of particulars in Texas, for example, and had lost thousands of dollars in sales. Apparently those publishers did not want to admit to censorship pressures in fear of losing more sales. Other publishers indicated that the censors would whitewash all textbooks if they could. They further indicated that if specific charges of the censoring organizations were disseminated to the general public, the censors would not wield so much power.

Publicity, then, is one answer to the censorship problem. Those people who would impose their beliefs on all others should be exposed. Those people who know exactly what should be taught in every academic subject at every grade level—and furthermore know exactly how it should be taught—should have their ideas exposed to the light of reason. Those people who object to virtually every story or poem in every basal reader should be asked to submit to the public the readers they would endorse. Then the censors should experience the close examination of their textbooks so that they might understand the problem from the other side of the desk.

Parents who are concerned about their children's education should demand a voice in the total educational process. They should ask to be placed on textbook selection committees, on curriculum committees, on decision-making committees. But before they request to do so, they should acquaint themselves with school problems and ask themselves if they can confront the problems objectively. They should further ask themselves whether or not they can place their own biases in a proper perspective as they examine school materials and course objectives.

Parents who want their children to grow up free to read, free to think, and free to make the critical decisions that will affect their lives must become involved. They dare not leave the business of the schools to the censors who have already become involved and who are attempting to make some drastic changes in the schools. Parents who believe in the Constitution and the Bill of Rights must begin reading and responding to bills affecting the schools that are introduced in their state legislatures and in Congress. Parents concerned about the rights of their children must be willing to protect those rights.

Freedom of speech, freedom to read, the right to know, and the right to teach are among the very first targets of totalitarian societies. Those freedoms have been severely challenged in the United States—particularly in the public schools. Concerned citizens must form groups to preserve those freedoms for the children of America rather than form groups to censor books.

Notes

Note: Not all citations contain complete information since the author received a number of newspaper clippings from friends throughout the country. The clippings did not always contain page numbers, dates, or other necessary information. And at least one of the clippings may have been attributed to the wrong newspaper.

Chapter One

1. Noel Rubinton in the *Indianapolis Star,* 2 July 1978, p. 1.
2. Ibid.
3. Ibid.
4. Larry Green in the *Los Angeles Times,* 3 June 1978, p. 1.
5. Rubinton, p. 20.
6. Green, p. 9.
7. Unless they are footnoted, the quotations in this chapter were recorded by the author in his visits to Warsaw.
8. *Warsaw Times-Union,* 12 April 1977, p. 3.
9. Ibid., 12 May 1977, p. 1.
10. Ibid., 24 May 1977, p. 9.
11. Ibid.
12. Ibid., 21 June 1977, p. 1.
13. Ibid., 12 July 1977, p. 1.
14. Minutes of the Meeting of the Board of School Trustees of the Warsaw Community Schools, 19 July 1977.
15. *Warsaw Times-Union,* 20 July 1977, p. 1.
16. Ibid., 9 August 1977, p. 3.
17. Ibid.
18. Minutes of the Meeting of the Board of School Trustees of the Warsaw Community Schools, 15 August 1977.
19. *Warsaw Times-Union,* 15 December 1977, p. 9.
20. Ibid., 9 August 1977, p. 3.
21. Minutes of the Meeting of the Board of School Trustees of the Warsaw Community Schools, 25 August 1977.
22. Supervisor's Conference Report to Teresa Burnau from C. J. Smith, 11 October 1977.
23. Ibid.
24. Staff Appraisal Criteria Supplemental Report on Teresa Burnau by C. J. Smith, 14 March 1978.
25. Letter to Teresa Burnau from Charles Bragg, 28 April 1978.
26. *KONTAC,* 26 May 1978, p. 2.
27. Ibid.
28. Minutes of a Special Session of the Board of School Trustees of the Warsaw Community Schools, 20 June 1977.

29. Ibid., 10 October 1977.
30. Memo to High School Teachers from C. J. Smith, 18 October 1977.
31. Minutes of the Meeting of the Board of Trustees of the Warsaw Community Schools, 9 January 1978.
32. Hearing Examiner's Report filed with the Indiana Education Employment Relations Board, 6 October 1978.
33. *Warsaw Times-Union,* 23 January 1978, p. 4.
34. Ibid., 13 June 1978, p. 3.
35. Ibid.
36. Ibid., p. 1.
37. Ibid., 14 June 1978, p. 4.
38. Ibid., 21 June 1978, p. 1.
39. Ibid., 21 June 1978, p. 18.
40. Ibid.
41. Report of Robert M. Lingenfelter to the Indiana Education Employment Relations Board, 6 October 1978, p. 13.

Chapter Two

1. "The Battle of the Books" is a title that several writers used to refer to the Kanawha County controversy. See footnotes 2 and 3 for examples.
2. John Egerton, "The Battle of the Books." *The Progressive,* June 1975, p. 13.
3. Franklin Parker, *The Battle of the Books: Kanawha County.* Bloomington, Ind.: The Phi Delta Kappa Educational Foundation, 1975. p. 8.
4. Ibid.
5. Ibid., p. 9.
6. James C. Hefley, *Textbooks on Trial.* Wheaton, Ill.: Victor Books, 1976. pp. 157, 160.
7. Egerton, p. 14.
8. Philip G. Jones, "A Clash over 'Dirty Books' Is Dividing a School Board, Threatening a Superintendent, and Shattering a Community." *The American School Board Journal* November 1974, p. 32.
9. Parker, p. 9.
10. Jones, p. 41.
11. Parker, p. 9.
12. Ibid., p. 10.
13. Jones, p. 41.
14. Ibid.
15. Ibid.
16. Ibid.
17. "A Brief Chronology of the West Virginia Textbook Crisis," *Arizona English Bulletin,* February 1975, p. 204.
18. *Charleston Daily Mail,* 11 September 1974, p. 1.
19. Ibid., 12 September 1974, p. 1.
20. "A Brief Chronology", p. 204.
21. Ibid.

22. Ibid.
23. Ibid., p. 205.
24. Ibid.
26. *Charleston Daily Mail,* 19 September 1974, p. 1.
27. Ibid., 23 September 1974, pp. 1, 4.
28. Ibid., 27 September 1974, p. 1.
29. "A Brief Chronology," p. 206.
30. Ibid.
31. Ibid.
32. Ibid.
33. Ibid., p. 207.
34. Ibid., p. 209.
35. Ibid.
36. Hefley, p. 166.
37. Ibid., p. 171.
38. "Administrative Regulation of the Kanawha County School System." Undated.
39. *Kanawha County, West Virginia: A Textbook Study in Cultural Conflict.* Washington, D.C.: National Education Association, 1975. pp. 34–35.
40. Ibid., p. 35.
41. Ibid.
42. Ibid., pp. 35–36
43. Ibid., p. 36.
44. Ibid., p. 23.
45. *The National Educator,* January 1978, p. 5.
46. Ibid.
47. Parker, p. 20.

Chapter Three

1. *Indianapolis Star,* 31 December 1978, p. 1.
2. *Los Angeles Times,* 3 June 1978, p. 1.
3. *Indianapolis Star,* 31 December 1978, p. 1.
4. Books pictured in an Associated Press photograph published in the *Indianapolis Star,* 31 December 1978, p. 1.
5. Ibid.
6. *The Asterisk: An Occasional Journal of English Traditions,* October 1978, p. 2.
7. Ibid.
8. Complaint filed in the Superior Court of the State of California in and for the County of Shasta for V. I. Wexner, et al. v. Anderson Union High School District Board of Trustees, p. 8.
9. Ibid., p. 9.
10. Ibid., p. 16.
11. *Los Angeles Times,* 23 September 1976, pt. VII, p. 1.
12. Ibid.

13. Xerox copy of a letter from the Culver City Board of Education to the Editor of the *Santa Monica Evening Outlook,* 1 October 1976.
14. Ibid.
15. Ibid.
16. *Oakland Tribune,* 11 January 1977, p. 1.
17. *San Francisco Chronicle* 13 January 1977, p. 10.
18. *Oakland Tribune,* 13 January 1977.
19. Ibid., 16 February 1977, p. 1.
20. *Newsletter on Intellectual Freedom,* March 1977, p. 46.
21. Complaint filed in the United States District Court for the District of Oregon for Nely L. Johnson, et al. v. Sedlen N. Stuart, et al., pp. 4–5.
22. Ibid., p. 7.
23. *Newsletter on Intellectual Freedom,* January 1978, pp. 8–9.
24. *Seattle Times,* 20 September 1978, p. H-1.
25. Ibid., 16 September 1978.
26. *Journal,* Rexburg, Idaho, 26 January 1978, p. 1.
27. Complaint filed in the United States District Court for the District of Idaho for John Fogarty v. Emma Atchley, et al., p. 6.
28. *Post-Register,* Idaho Falls, 24 January 1978, p. B-10.
29. Fogarty complaint, p. 6.
30. *Newsletter on Intellectual Freedom,* November 1978, p. 137.
31. Ibid., May 1978, p. 57.
32. Ibid., November 1978, p. 138.
33. Ibid.
34. Ibid., pp. 137–138.
35. *Chicago Sun-Times,* 14 November 1973, p. 40.
36. Ibid.
37. Ibid., 18 November 1973, p. 14.
38. *Censorship News,* March 1975, p. 4.
39. Ibid., September 1975, p. 10.
40. *Newsletter on Intellectual Freedom,* May 1978, p. 56.
41. *Morning Advocate,* Baton Rouge, Louisiana, 16 January 1975, p. 1-B.
42. Ibid.
43. Ibid., 11 March 1975, p. 1.
44. *Daily Reveille,* Baton Rouge, Louisiana, 25 September 1975, p. 8.
45. *Morning Advocate,* 19 September 1975.
46. Ibid.
47. *Daily Reveille,* 25 September 1975, p. 8.
48. *Morning Advocate,* 30 April 1975, p. 1-B.
49. *Newsletter on Intellectual Freedom,* March 1977, p. 36.
50. Ibid.
51. Ibid., September 1977, p. 134.
52. *Clayton County Register,* 20 April 1977, p. 1.
53. Page 4, paragraph 4 of the remarks of Mrs. Robert Sage to a meeting of the school board of the Central Community School District of Elkader, Iowa, 19 April 1977.

54. I compared the text of Mrs. Robert Sage's speech with the reviews of the Ginn 360 Reading Series distributed by Educational Research Analysts.
55. *Clayton County Register,* p. 1.
56. *Cedar Rapids Gazette,* 28 April 1977, p. 1.
57. *Newsletter on Intellectual Freedom,* March 1978, p. 30.
58. Ibid., May 1978, p. 56.
59. Ibid., p. 65.
60. Ibid., March 1977, p. 37.
61. *Minneapolis Star,* 6 May 1977, p. 13-A.
62. Ibid.
63. *Newsletter on Intellectual Freedom,* March 1978, p. 31.
64. Ibid., July 1978, p. 89.
65. Ibid., November 1978, p. 138.
66. *Bulletin,* Forest Lake, Minnesota, 29 June 1978.
67. Letters to Edward Jenkinson from two teachers in Minnesota.
68. Ibid.
69. *Newsletter on Intellectual Freedom,* March 1977, p. 37.
70. The guidelines were distributed at a meeting in the high school cafeteria of Park Rapids, Minnesota, 17 January 1977.

Chapter Four

1. *Milwaukee Journal,* 9 April 1978, p. 1.
2. Ibid.
3. Ibid., p. 20.
4. *Lake County Reporter,* Hartland, Wisconsin, 21 February 1978, p. 1.
5. *Capital Times,* Madison, Wisconsin, 24 April 1978.
6. Ibid., 27 April 1978.
7. *Wausau Daily Herald,* 19 January 1978.
8. *Green-Bay Press-Gazette,* 28 February 1978.
9. Ibid., 15 March 1978, p. 7.
10. *Waukesha Freeman,* 15 February 1978.
11. Ibid.
12. Ibid., 26 April 1978.
13. *Milwaukee Journal,* 22 February 1978.
14. Ibid.
15. Ibid., 24 March 1978.
16. *Newsletter on Intellectual Freedom,* September 1977, p. 133.
17. Ibid.
18. Ibid.
19. *Washington Post,* 17 March 1978.
20. *Newsletter on Intellectual Freedom,* September 1978, p. 119.
21. Ibid., p. 118.
22. Ibid., March 1974, p. 32.
23. *Atlanta Journal,* 27 May 1977.
24. *Newsletter on Intellectual Freedom,* July 1978, p. 87.

25. Ibid., March 1974, p. 33.
26. Ibid., November 1974, p. 156.
27. Ibid., September 1978, p. 119.
28. *Herndon Tribune,* 13 March 1975, p. 1.
29. Ibid., p. 15.
30. *Newsletter on Intellectual Freedom,* March 1978, p. 30.
31. Ibid., p. 31.
32. Ibid., p. 39.
33. Ibid.
34. Ibid., September 1977, p. 133.
35. Ibid., July 1978, p. 88.
36. Ibid., September 1978, p. 123.
37. Ibid., March 1977, p. 37.
38. *Bradford Era,* 14 March 1977.
39. *Newsletter on Intellectual Freedom,* November 1977, p. 156.
40. Ibid., pp. 155, 163.
41. *Daily Item,* Sunbury, Pennsylvania, 23 November 1977, p. 5.
42. Ibid.
43. Ibid., 19 April 1977, p. 21.
44. Ibid., 9 September 1977.
45. Ibid., 12 August 1977, p. 3.
46. *Newsletter on Intellectual Freedom,* July 1978, p. 98.
47. Ibid.
48. Ibid., March 1977, p. 46.
49. Ibid., July 1978, p. 94.
50. *Philadelphia Inquier,* 3 April 1977, B-1, B-4.
51. *Newsletter on Intellectual Freedom,* November 1977, p. 155.
52. News release prepared by the United Teachers of Island Trees, October 7, 1976, p. 1.
53. Ibid., p. 2.
54. Ibid.
55. *Newsletter on Intellectual Freedom,* March 1977, pp. 45, 59.
56. Brief of American Jewish Committee, American Jewish Congress, Anti-Defamation League of B'nai B'rith, The American Orthopsychiatric Association, The Ethical Humanist Society of Long Island, Long Island Council of Churches, The National Council of Teachers of English, The Unitarian Universalist Association and Writers in the Public Interest, submitted in the United States District Court for the Eastern District of New York in the case of Steven A. Pico, by his next friend, Frances Pico, et al., Plaintiffs, against Board of Education, Island Trees Union Free School District, et al., Defendants, p. 7.
57. Ibid.
58. *Newsletter on Intellectual Freedom,* March 1978, p. 31.
59. *School Bell,* a publication of the National Congress for Educational Excellence, May-June 1978, p. 4.

60. *Newsletter on Intellectual Freedom,* May 1978, p. 57.
61. *School Bell,* p. 4.
62. Ibid., January-February 1978, p. 5.
63. Ibid.
64. *Newsletter on Intellectual Freedom,* March 1977, p. 37.
65. *Boston Sunday Globe,* 20 March 1977, p. 35.
66. *Times Record,* New Brunswick, Maine, 27 September 1977, p. 1.
67. Ibid., p. 21.
68. *Newsletter on Intellectual Freedom,* September 1978, p. 119.
69. Ibid.
70. *School Bell,* May-June 1978, p. 4.
71. Ibid.
72. *Newsletter on Intellectual Freedom,* September 1977, p. 134.

Chapter Five

1. Mel Gabler, "Have you read your child's school textbooks?" *Faith for the Family,* March-April, 1974, p. 4. (The page number refers to a reprint distributed by Educational Research Analysts.)
2. *Milwaukee Journal,* 6 November 1978, p. 1.
3. *South Bend Tribune,* 17 October 1978, p. 17.
4. *Indianapolis Star,* 31 December 1978, p. 1.
5. *Kanawha County, West Virginia: A Textbook Study in Cultural Conflict.* Washington, D.C.: National Education Association, 1975. p. 41.
6. Franklin Parker, *The Battle of the Books: Kanawha County.* Bloomington, Ind.: The Phi Delta Kappa Educational Foundation, 1975. p. 26.
7. *Minneapolis Tribune,* 24 September 1978, p. 1-E.
8. Ken Donelson, "Censorship: Some Issues and Problems." *Theory into Practice,* June 1975, p. 193.
9. Lester Asheim, "Not Censorship but Selection." *Wilson Library Bulletin,* September 1953, p. 67.

Chapter Six

1. *The American Heritage Dictionary of the English Language.* Boston: American Heritage Publishing Co. and Houghton Mifflin, 1969. p. 117.
2. *Newsletter on Intellectual Freedom,* September 1976, pp. 115–116.
3. Ibid., November 1976, p. 145.
4. Ibid., January 1977, p. 7.
5. *St. Louis Post-Dispatch,* 18 April 1977, p. 1.
6. Report of the Texas Commissioner of Education to the State Board of Education, 12–13 November 1976.
7. Undated Bill of Particulars submitted to the Texas Commissioner of Education by the "Textbook Chairman" of the Texas Society of the Daughters of the American Revolution.
8. Ibid.

9. The words listed herein are taken from five bills of particulars submitted to the Texas Commissioner of Education in July of 1976.
10. Response filed by Prentice-Hall, Inc., to a specific bill of particulars asking that *Webster's New World Dictionary* not be adopted in Texas in 1976.
11. Bill of Particulars submitted to the Teaxs Commissioner of Education on July 9, 1976 by the Texas NOW Continuing Task Force for Education for Women.
12. *Teacher Advocate*, Official Publication of the Indiana State Teachers Association, January-February 1979, p. 16.
13. Mel Gabler on *The Phil Donahue Show*, 16 January 1978.
14. Mel Gabler in a mimeographed handout for parents concerned about values clarification.
15. Mimeographed outline entitled Textbook Reviewing by Categories. The outline was included in a packet of materials that the Gablers sent to a concerned parent.
16. Mimeographed review distributed by the Gablers entitled *The Ginn 360 Reading Series—A Critical Analysis* by Mrs. Evelyn Parise, C. P. F. member from Winterville, Ohio. p. 3.
17. Mimeographed review distributed by the Gablers entitled TO TURN A STONE/Ginn and Company/1970/READING/6th grade, p. 1.
18. Mimeographed review distributed by the Gablers entitled MAN THE MYTH-MAKER/Literature, Uses of the Imagination/Harcourt/1973/High School/Student's Edition/Review by Mosby, p. 15.
19. Letter dated August 9, 1974, to Dr. M. L. Brockette, Texas Education Agency, Capitol Station, Austin, Texas, from the Mel Gablers. A mimeographed copy of the letter, which serves as a bill of particulars in the Texas State Textbook Adoption process, was included in the packet that the Gablers mailed to a concerned parent who had requested reviews of the Ginn 360 Reading Series.
20. TO TURN A STONE/p. 8.
21. Brockette letter, p. 15.
22. MAN THE MYTH-MAKER/p. 24.
23. Mimeographed review distributed by the Gablers entitled Specific Objections to Ginn, p. 14.
24. Mimeographed review distributed by the Gablers entitled Man in Literature—Comparative World Studies in Translation/1970/High School/Student's and Teacher's books/Mosby, p. 1.
25. TO TURN A STONE/p. 4.
26. SPECIFIC OBJECTIONS, p. 16.
27. TO TURN A STONE/p. 4.
28. Mimeographed review distributed by the Gablers entitled *MARQUEE*, Man in Literature Series, "Noon Wine", A play by Sam Peckinpah, p. 1.
29. Brockette letter, p. 17.
30. Ibid., p. 15.
31. Ibid., p. 20.

32. Ibid.
33. Ibid., p. 25.
34. Ibid.
35. TO TURN A STONE/p. 6.
36. Ibid., p. 8.
37. SPECIFIC OBJECTIONS, p. 1.
38. Ibid., p. 14.

Chapter Seven

1. The Honorable John R. Rarick, "Public Education a Victim of Liberal Revolution," *Congressional Record,* 15 July 1971. (Reprint distributed by The Network of Patriotic Letter Writers.)
2. Georgina Schreiber, "A Christian Mother's View of the Values Clarification Program." Baton Rouge, La.: Concerned Citizens and Taxpayers for Decent School Books.
3. *Barbara M. Morris Report,* June 1974, p. 6.
4. Onalee McGraw, "Secular Humanism and the Schools: The Issue Whose Time Has Come," *Critical Issues Series 2.* Washington, D.C.: The Heritage Foundation, 1976. pp. 19–20.
5. James C. Hefley, *Textbooks on Trial.* Wheaton, Ill.: Victor Books, 1976. p. 209.
6. Mary Royer, "Humanism—a clear-cut philosophy," *Public Education: River of Pollution.* Fullerton, Ca.: Educator Publications. (The article was reprinted and distributed by Young Parents Alert.)
7. John Steinbacher, "To Capture a Nation—Change the Religion," p. 1. (The reprint which was distributed by Young Parents Alert did not identify the source of the article; however, Mr. Steinbacher is managing editor of *The National Educator* in Fullerton, California.)
8. Torcaso v. Watkins, Clerk, 367 U.S. 488 (1961).
9. Ibid., p. 489.
10. Ibid., p. 495.
11. Ibid.
12. United States v. Seeger, 380 U.S. 163 (1965).
13. Ibid., p. 187.
14. Ibid., p. 174.
15. Ibid., p. 193.
16. Ibid., pp. 192–193.
17. Fellowship of Humanity v. County of Alameda, 153 C.A. 2d 673; 315 P. 2d 394.
18. Ibid., pp. 690–691.
19. Ibid., pp. 678–679.
20. "Secularism," *New Catholic Encylopedia* (1967), XIII, p. 36.
21. "Humanist Manifesto II," *The Humanist,* September-October 1973, pp. 5–8.
22. Unsigned mimeographed sheet distributed by Educational Research Analysts, Parents of Minnesota, Inc., and Young Parents Alert among other organizations.

23. "Guide to Humanistic Terminology," *School Bell* (a publication of the National Congress for Educational Excellence), January-February 1978, p. 6. (The guide is being distributed by at least four other organizations.)
24. John Rarick, "Public Education"
25. *Barbara M. Morris Report.*

Chapter Eight

1. See dust jacket of James C. Hefley's *Textbooks on Trial.* Wheaton, Ill.: Victor Books, 1976.
2. Mimeographed sheet distributed by the Gablers entitled PARENT GROUPS.
3. Mel Gabler, "Have you read your child's school textbooks?" *Faith for the Family,* March-April, 1974. p. 4. (Page number refers to the reprint distributed by Educational Research Analysts.)
4. Printed sheet entitled "The Mel Gablers Educational Research Analysts," November 1977.
5. Printed sheet entitled "THE MEL GABLERS—Consumer Advocates for Education."
6. Mimeographed sheet distributed by the Gablers entitled "FOR YOUR CONSIDERATION. . ."
7. "THE MEL GABLERS".
8. Mimeographed sheet distributed by the Gablers entitled 1978 Report and mailed in November of 1978. p. 2.
9. Ibid.
10. Associated Press dispatch published in the *Temple Daily Telegraph,* Temple, Texas.
11. Ibid.
12. Ibid.
13. *Longview* (Texas) *Morning Journal,* 13 September 1970, p. 4-A.
14. *Newport* (Vermont) *Daily Express,* 7 May 1975.
15. *Vermont Sunday News,* 30 September 1973, p. 1.
16. *Borger* (Texas) *News-Herald,* 14 November 1972, p. 1.
17. Baltimore *News American,* 19 May 1975.
18. *Burlington* (Vermont) *Free Press,* 17 October 1975.
19. Reprint T-413 distributed by the Gablers.
20. *South Bend Tribune,* 25 September 1978.
21. Publication T-465 and a mimeographed sheet entitled 1978 Report distributed by the Gablers.
22. Hefley, *Textbooks.*
23. Mimeographed strip of paper included by the Gablers in packets sent to concerned parents.
24. Ibid.
25. Letter dated August 9, 1974, to Dr. M. L. Brockette, Texas Education Agency, Capitol Station, Austin, Texas, from the Mel Gablers. A mimeographed copy of the letter was included in a packet that the Gablers mailed

173

to a concerned parent since he requested reviews of the Ginn 360 Reading Series.

26. Specific objections in the mimeographed letter have been stamped "This Section replaced in Texas adoption" or "Deleted or changed for Texas adoption."

27. Twelve-page letter to the Texas Commissioner of Education from the Gablers, 8 August 1974.

28. Twenty-two page letter to the Texas Commissioner of Education from the Gablers, 9 August 1972.

29. Mimeographed publication of the Gablers entitled Current Activities, September 1978.

Chapter Nine

1. *Educational Signpost,* December 1972, p. 1.

2. Mimeographed sheet entitled "The Fact Finding Committee Concerning Classroom Sex Education," p. 1.

3. Ibid., p. 2.

4. Ibid.

5. Mimeographed letters to and from Cathryn Dorney, Executive Director of AEA. Dates of letters: January 1976; 1 October 1976; March 1978.

6. *The American Education Association Gets into the Anti E.R. A. Debate Spurred on by Interview with Cathryn L. K. Dorney.* New York: American Education Association, 1977.

7. America's Future, "200 recommended social studies texts," Fall 1977, p. 16.

8. The statement is printed on the last page of each four-page Textbook Evaluation Report distributed by America's Future.

9. ALEC, 1977 Suggested State Legislation, p. 1.

10. Ibid.

11. Ibid., p. 49.

12. Onalee McGraw, *Secular Humanism and the Schools: The Issue Whose Time Has Come.* Washington, D.C.: The Heritage Foundation, 1976. p. 4.

13. ALEC, p. 51.

14. Ibid., p. 52.

15. Ibid., p. 57.

16. Ibid., pp. 58–59.

17. Ibid., p. 60.

18. Charles Park, "Clouds on the Right: A Review of Pending Pressures Against Education," in James David, ed., *Dealing with Censorship.* Urbana, Ill.: The National Council of Teachers of English, 1979.

19. Robert Welch, *What Is the John Birch Society?* Belmont, Mass.: The John Birch Society, 1970.

20. *Kanawha County, West Virginia: A Textbook Study in Cultural Conflict.* Washington, D.C.: National Education Association, 1975.

21. Alan Stang, "The N.E.A., Dictatorship of the Educariat." Reprint of article published in *American Opinion Magazine,* p. 12.

22. Undated printed sheet entitled "Introducing the Racism and Sexism Center for Educators." Council on Interracial Books for Children.
23. Undated printed sheet introducing *Human Values in Children's Books.* Council on Interracial Books for Children.
24. Undated printed sheet introducing *Stereotypes, Distortions and Omissions in U.S. History Textbooks.* Council on Interracial Books for Children.
25. "Introducing the Racism".
26. Undated membership flier for The Eagle Forum.
27. Ibid.
28. *Phyllis Schlafly Report,* December 1976, p. 4.
29. Undated mimeographed letter from GEM to "Friends of Maine's young people."
30. Ibid.
31. "Fact Sheet Concerning Health Education for Maine Schools," 22 April 1978.
32. Letter from GEM.
33. Undated printed sheet entitled "The Heritage Foundation: Introduction."
34. Headlines from *Education Update,* September 1977 and Winter 1978.
35. *Education Update,* September 1977, p. 6.
36. McGraw, p. ii.
37. Ibid., p. 17.
38. Onalee McGraw, *Family Choice in Education: The New Imperative.* Washington, D.C.: The Heritage Foundation, 1978. p. 50.
39. Undated mimeographed publication of the Indiana Education Coalition, p. 1.
40. Printed information sheet distributed by LITE, 14 November 1977, p. 2.
41. Ibid., pp. 1–2.
42. Masthead of the *School Bell,* official publication of the National Congress for Educational Excellence.
43. Joanne McAuley, "President's Note Pad," *School Bell,* March-April 1978, p. 2.
44. Mimeographed membership form distributed by PARENTS.
45. "Parenting," PARENTS, November 1978, p. 1.
46. Jil Wilson, "Parenting: A Report for Parents," PARENTS, November 1978, p. 4.
47. Membership brochure of Parents of Minnesota, Inc.
48. *Minneapolis Tribune,* 24 September 1978, p. 1-E.
49. Ibid., p. 4-E.
50. Ibid.
51. Mimeographed announcement of the Third Annual Education Seminar, 30 September 1978, in St. Paul, Minnesota.
52. Mimeographed letter addressed to "Dear Friend of Family Rights" from Mae Duggan, President, March 1977.
53. *St. Louis Review,* 18 March 1977.
54. Ibid.

Chapter Ten

1. Radio Station WHA—Madison devoted *The Wisconsin Issues Forum* to a discussion of censorship on December 17, 1978. Jil Wilson represented PARENTS. The author was one of the invited panelists who opposed the censorship of school materials.
2. Mailloux v. Kiley, 436 F. 2d 565 (1st Cir.), *after dismissal,* 323 F. Supp. 1387 (D. Mass.), *aff'd,* 448 F. 2d 1242 (1st Cir. 1971) (per curiam).
3. David Rubin, *The Rights of Teachers: An American Civil Liberties Union Handbook.* New York: Avon Books, 1971.
4. Maillous v. Kiley, 323 F. Supp. 1392.
5. Ibid.
6. Ibid.
7. Ibid.
8. Stephen R. Goldstein, "The Asserted Constitutional Right of Public School Teachers to Determine What They Teach." University of Pennsylvania Law Review 124: 1293–1357, June 1976, p. 1324.
9. Ibid., p. 1326.
10. Ibid., p. 1329.
11. Ibid., pp. 1355–1356.
12. Ibid., p. 1356.
13. Bob Cary, et al. v. Board of Education of the Adams-Arapahoe School District 28-J, Aurora, Colorado, 427 F. Supp. 945, 952 (D. Colo. 1977).
14. Ibid., p. 3. (Page numbers refer to mimeographed copy of the decision.)
15. Ibid.
16. Ibid., pp. 15–16.
17. Ibid., p. 16.
18. Ibid., p. 13.
19. Ibid., p. 14.
20. Ibid., p. 21.
21. Ibid.
22. Keefe v. Geanakos, 418 F. 2d 359 (1st Cir. 1969).
23. Parducci v. Rutland, 316 F. Supp. 352 (M.D. Ala. 1970).
24. Wieman v. Updegragg, 344 U.S. 183.
25. Parducci, pp. 353–54.
26. Ibid.
27. Ibid., pp. 355–356.
28. Ibid., p. 356.
29. Tinker v. Des Moines Independent Community School District, 393 U.S. 503 (1969).
30. Sterzing v. Fort Bend Independent School District, 376 F. Supp. 657 (1972).
31. Ibid.
32. Ibid.
33. State ex rel. Wailewski v. Board of School Directors, 14 Wus. 2d 243, 111 N. W. 2d 198 (1961).

34. Ahern v. Board of Education, 327 F. Supp. 1391 (D. Neb. 1971), *aff'd,* 456 F. 2d 399 (8th Cir. 1972).
35. Birdwell v. Hazel School District, 352 F. Supp. 613 (E.D. Mo. 1972), *aff'd,* 491 F. 2d 490 (8th Cir. 1974).
36. Adams v. Campbell County School District, 511 F. 2d 1242 (10th Cir. 1975).
37. Parker v. Board of Education, 237 F. Supp. 222 (D. Md.), *aff'd,* 348 F. 2d 464 (4th Cir. 1965).
38. Sheldon H. Nahmod, "Controversy in the Classroom: The High School Teacher and Freedom of Expression." George Washington Law Review 39: 1031, July 1974.
39. Julia Turnquist Bradley, "Censoring the School Library: Do Students Have the Right to Read?" Connecticut Law Review 10: 747–774, Spring 1978, p. 767.
40. Robert M. O'Neil, "Libraries, Liberty and the First Amendment." University of Cincinnati Law Review 42: 209–252, No. 2, 1973, p. 209.
41. Ibid., pp. 209–210.
42. President's Council, District 25 v Community School Board No. 25, 457 F. 2d 293 (2d Cir. 1972).
43. Ibid.
44. 409 U.S. 999–1000 (1972).
45. O'Neil, p. 212.
46. Ibid., p. 252.
47. Minarcini v. Strongsville City School District, 384 F. Supp. 698, *aff'd,* 541 F. 2d 577 (6th Cir. 1976).
48. Ibid., p. 581.
49. *The United States Law Week,* 30 August 1976, p. 2132.
50. Ibid.
51. Ibid.
52. Right to Read Defense Committee of Chelsea, et al. v. School Committee of the City of Chelsea, et al. (Notes taken from mimeographed copy of Judge Tauro's decision, p. 8.)
53. Ibid.
54. Ibid., pp. 8–9.
55. Jody Caravaglia, "The City to a Young Girl," reprinted in *Male and Female Under 18.*
56. *Right to Read,* p. 10.
57. Ibid., p. 16.
58. Ibid., p. 19.
59. Ibid., pp. 35–36.

Chapter Eleven

1. *Newsletter on Intellectual Freedom,* May 1973, p. 52.
2. Ibid.
3. Ibid., January 1978, p. 8.

4. Ibid., November 1976, p. 145.
5. Ibid., p. 146.
6. Ibid., January 1977, p. 7.
7. Ibid., September 1976, p. 116.
8. Ibid., January 1979, p. 5.
9. Ibid., September 1974, p. 111.
10. Ibid., May 1975, p. 77.
11. Ibid., July 1975, pp. 103, 108.
12. Ibid., May 1977, p. 73.

Index

179

Index

Index

Mahwah, N.J., 59
Making It with Mademoiselle, 82
Male and Female Under 18, 57, 153–54
Man: A Course of Study, 112–15, 126, 135
Manchild in the Promised Land, 158
Man in Literature, 90
Man the Myth-maker, 89
Manton, Mich., 42
Mass Media and the Popular Arts, 38
"Mateo Falcone," 109
McBroom's Zoo, 57
Middletown, Md., 56
"Miller's Tale, The," 80
Milton-Freewater, Ore., 33
Minnesota Civil Liberties Union, 44
Montgomery County, Md., 56–57, 157
Monticello, Iowa, 42
Moon Children, The, 60
Ms., 62
Multi-Cultural Non-Sexist Advisory Committee of Cedar Rapids, The, 157
My Darling, My Hamburger, 83

Naked Ape, The, 39, 60
Naomi in the Middle, 60
Nashua, N.H., 62
National Coalition for Children, 126, 133
National Congress for Educational Excellence 126, 135–36; and humanistic education, 64, 106; involvement in New Hampshire, 62
National Education Association, 24, 26, 128, 160
National Education Association Inquiry Panel, 26–27
National Educator, The, 126, 141
National Federation of American Party Women, 126
National Geographic, 36
National Organization for Women, 56, 69, 81, 141, 157
National Rifle Association, 122
National Science Foundation, 112
National Traditional Caucus, 126
Native Son, 59
Network of Patriotic Letter Writers, The, 96, 106–7, 141

New American Poetry 1945–1960, 145
New Catholic Encyclopedia, 102
"New Fence, The," 88
New Hanover County, N.C., 54–55
New Lisbon, Maine, 63–64
New Women: A Motive Anthology of Women's Liberation, The, 6
Newport Daily Express, 110
News American, 112
Newsweek, 36, 87
Not Bad for a Girl, 38

Oakland, Calif., 32–33
". . . Of An Organization," 93
Office for Intellectual Freedom, xviii, 29, 160
Of Mice and Men, 57, 62, 73, 156
Oil City, Pa., 57
Oliver Twist, 30
One Flew Over the Cuckoo's Nest, 35
On the Edge, 90, 94
Oregon State Textbook Commission, 33
Orphan, The, 60
Our Bodies, Ourselves, 36–37, 62
Outsiders, The, 83

Parents and Taxpayers, 126
Parents of Minnesota, Inc., 43, 45–49, 70, 137–38
Parents of New York—United, 60, 126, 141
Parents Resisting Invasion of Rights in Training Youth, 126
Parents Rights, Inc., 139
Parents Who Care, 56, 141
Park Rapids, Minn., 45–49, 86
People Make a Nation, The, 119, 121
People of America Responding to Educational Needs of Today's Society, 66, 67, 136–37, 142
People Who Care, 13, 66–67, 141
Peru, Ill., 53
Philadelphia, Pa., 57–58
Phyllis Schlafly Report, The, 130
Pigman, The, 83
Pill Versus the Springhill Mine Disaster, The, 30
Pinellas County, Fla., 54
"Pocket Guide to Unitarianism," 101
Portland, Ore., 33–34

Index

183

Index